St. Catte's Academy for Kittens

St. Catte's Academy - for Kittens

Moira Bates

Paperback Edition First Published in the United Kingdom
in 2016 by aSys Publishing

Copyright © Moira Bates

Moira Bates has asserted her rights under 'the Copyright Designs and Patents
Act 1988' to be identified as the author of this work.

Disclaimer

This is a work of fiction. Names, characters, businesses, places, events and
incidents are either the products of the author's imagination or used in a fictitious
manner. Any resemblance to actual persons, living or dead, or actual events is
purely coincidental.

ISBN: 978-1-910757-76-5

aSys Publishing
http://www.asys-publishing.co.uk

St. Catte's Academy for Kittens

ST. CATTE'S ACADEMY

The premier Independent School for kittens

PROSPECTUS

At **St. Catte's**, we aim to provide the all-round education which will enable every kitten to achieve her full potential. We combine a relaxed approach with a passion for learning and a real sense of purpose.

Classes augment the National Curriculum

- Excellent teaching
- Progressive teaching style
- Individual Learning Programmes
- Friendly and welcoming atmosphere
- Caring yet stimulating environment
- Bursaries and scholarships available
- Extensive grounds
- Sporting excellence
- Successful choir

St. Catte's is a charitable trust

Head : Dr. Tabitha Feline CBE

Principuss,

St. Catte's Academy.

Catterham Way,

Purrley,

PU55IE

In partnership with the St. Thomas College for tom-cat kittens

ST. CATTE'S ACADEMY

Welcome to St. Catte's, the foremost Independent School for the education of young cats. Our aim is to launch happy and confident kittens, every one capable of reaching her own potential in life. Each of our kittens graduates with the ability to teach her Human how to provide a comfortable and well organised home. A well-trained Human is a happy Human, with a happy cat.

The Old School House is a traditional building: a grey stone manor house set in its own grounds and once the home of minor Royalty. Wood panelling and the carved central staircase in the entrance hall provide a gracious setting in which both staff and pupils are housed. All meals are taken in the dining room.

Classes take place in the modern educational environment of the New School, situated across the courtyard.

Principuss: Dr. Tabitha Feline CBE, St. Catte's Academy, Catterham Way, Purrley, London.

PLEASE NOTE THAT THE LIBRARY HAS BEEN BOOKED FOR THE

GOVERNORS' MEETING AT 6.30 THIS EVENING

Handwritten note : from Dr. Tabitha Feline, Head.

TO ALL STAFF: As we agreed, the Fifth Years will be responsible for supervising this evening's Activity Session. The Sixth Years will welcome the Governors as they arrive, and will assist Mrs. Catford with refreshments during the meeting. Tabitha Feline

SIXTH FORM TEXTS

Immi # KITTEN ALERT main staircase

Sam # on my way

Rosie # MAYDAY Top landing. Little beggars are swarming

Yaz # Gridlock situation bottom of stairs

Zo # OMG BIG TROUBLE WITCHSPITZ IN SIGHT

Memo from: Ms. T. W. Spitz

To : Dr. Tabitha Feline

URGENT - <u>Time 7.30 p.m.</u>

I left late this evening to find a dreadful commotion going on in the Main Hall, with 1st and 2nd Year kittens running about up and down the main staircase chasing small spots of light created by a giggling group of what appeared to be Fifth Years, hanging over the balcony rail on the first landing. The Sixth Years were nowhere to be seen. I assume the uproar did not disturb you at the Governors' Meeting in the Library, but it would have reflected badly on the School had you all come down from the Meeting at that time. **I am bringing this to your attention by leaving it on your desk, as you can see, because I feel sure you will wish to deal with it at once.**

Tristia W. Spitz

Handwritten Note no. 1 to MS. SPITZ from Dr. Tabitha Feline

Thank you for drawing last night's over-exuberance to my attention, and I'm sorry you were so late going home. I have attached my notes from the Governors' Meeting for your information. As expected, the decision was taken to computerise our admin. system. The vote was unanimous, I'm afraid. Would you type up the attached and take them around to all Tutors asap. Thanks.

MEMO: TO ALL FORM TUTORS *from Tabitha Feline*

URGENT: *Please display the following notice in every Form Room and draw the attention of EACH KITTEN to its contents. Thank you.*

<u>NOTICE - *for typing*</u>

Will the kittens (I suspect the Fifth Years) who used light-pen laser torches to amuse the kitlets during the evening activity hour - KINDLY DESIST. The 1st and 2nd Year pupils were getting thoroughly over-excited chasing the light-spots and pouncing upon each other in unseemly rugby scrums resulting in kitten pile-ups in the main Hall, and generally causing chaos.

I DO NOT WISH TO SEE THIS HAPPEN AGAIN. The instigators of any over-exuberant bout of exercise in the evenings will be given the task of calming the kitlets down, and getting them off to sleep.

Tabitha Feline

QUICK NOTE to Pawlene McFurley, Deputy Head and Polly Purrkins, Matron from Tabitha Feline.

What will they come up with next!! Now all the excitement has died down and the laser-pens confiscated, we can take time to look at occupying the Year Fives. I like your idea of giving them responsibility for organising the pre-supper activity then settling the kitlets down. Discuss over a glass of sherry later? T.

Handwritten Note no. 2 to MISS SPITZ *from Dr. Tabitha Feline :*

As you know, in the post this morning I received written confirmation of the Governors' decision on the need for updating our office systems, and they have therefore approved funding for the purchase of the computer and all training required for its use. I'm afraid we can't delay the project any longer. Perhaps you would join me for coffee later, when we can talk it all over?

Would you type up the attached and get them off as soon as possible. Thanks.

1. **Memo to ALL STAFF.**

The School Governors have recommended that our admin. procedures are updated as soon as possible. They have therefore approved the purchase of a computer and any necessary training. I will supply further details at the Staff Meeting.

2. **LETTER to Purry's Electronics, address and FAO as attached quotation.**

With reference to your recent visit to the School and our subsequent telephone conversation, please supply computer and accessories as detailed in the attached specification. We will require the training package which was included in the quotation.

Please contact Ms. Spitz, our School Secretary, to arrange details of delivery and installation.

Yrs. etc.

*Handwritten note no. 3 to MS. SPITZ from
Dr. Tabitha Feline :*

*As we discussed yesterday, I do hope you will consider undertaking
the computer training. It is no longer possible to delay updating our
admin systems to bring them into line with the computer age*

*Communication has moved on, as the Governors have pointed out,
and we have no option but to move with the times.*

Perhaps we can discuss it over lunch?

Tabitha Feline

Email from ENID PURRSEY TO HER MOTHER :

From enid.p.@setnet.com

To l.purrsey@vsc.net

Subj. AAAARGH!!!!!!

Dear Mum, sorry I missed your call. Working late. He's still loading HIS
work on to ME and still won't give me a rise. Fed up.

Might see you Friday. Love E.

QUICK NOTE to Pawlene McFurley, Deputy Head from Dr. Tabitha Feline

*As anticipated, Miss Spitz is not taking kindly to the prospect of the
computer.*

*Would you chat with some of the younger members of staff. They
might have ideas about how to present all this in a favourable light.
Thanks. T.*

SIXTH FORM TEXTS

Rosie # don't report yr lost key. Witch Spitz in a right paddy

Immi # so wot's new abt that

Rosie # nearly bit my head off

Zo # heard Catfood tell Matron Witch Spitz might b leaving

Rosie # wot?

Immi # wot?

Yaz # wot?

Sam # wot?

Zo # big meeting WitchSpitz/Ms Tabitha first thing ths mng

Yaz # coo. Ears to the ground y'all

Sam # report back at lunch

LETTER TO DR. TABITHA FELINE FROM MS. SPITZ

TRISTIA W. SPITZ

Dr. Tabitha Feline,

St. Catte's Academy.

Dear Dr. Tabitha,

It is with regret that I confirm our conversation of this morning. If the Governors feel that the administration procedures I have inaugurated are no longer adequate without being computerised, I feel that I have no option but to tender my resignation. Please thank them for their kind offer of computer training courses, which I decline. I do not feel inclined to 'update my skills', as you put it, to reorganise a system which has to date proved entirely successful. A typewriter and a telephone are sufficient technology for an experienced office manager.

I did not reach this decision without much thought and shall miss being the vital hub at the heart of the St. Catte's team. However, I feel that it will be better for all concerned if I leave without delay.

Yours sincerely,

Tristia W. Spitz

SIXTH FORM TEXTS

Rosie # to Yaz #, Sam #, Zo #, Immi # Witchspitz deffo going! Thank pawd for that!!

Zo # OMG wot happened, i didn't think we'd ever get rid of her

Sam # Yay, lets raid the stationery cupboard and liberate the pens and hand out paper, wot happened

Rosie # dunno, something to do with a computer, refused to go on the IT course or something

Yaz # OMG, imagine life without witchspitz snooping

Sam # no more having your calls listened in on

Immi # appawlling grammar but i know wot you mean!!

Yaz # gotta go, c u at lunch

ADVERTISEMENT

ST. CATTE'S ACADEMY

The premier Independent School for kittens

Required : SCHOOL SECRETARY/PERSONAL ASSISTANT

Principuss: Dr. Tabitha Feline, CBE,

St. Catte's Academy,

Catterham Way, Purrley, PU55IE. Telephone: 01737 446879

SIXTH FORM TEXTS

Sam # to Rosie, Zo, Immi and Yaz # Hv volunteered us for general duties on the interview afternoon. Mrs. Catfords making loadsa cake. Yay!!!!

Email to : ENID PURRSEY FROM HER MOTHER:

To enid@setnet.com **from l.purrsey@vsc.net**

Subject: Job

Dear Enid. Your Auntie Daphne says they need a PA at St. Catte's, Purrley. She'll text you the number. Ring and say that you're interested. I think she knows the Matron there. Don't ask - Daphne knows everyone!!! The Head's name is Dr. Tabitha Feline and she's expecting a call from you. Love Mum

Email to : l.purrsey@vsc.net

From enid.p.@setnet.com

Subj. Job

Dear Mum. Wow! Long 'phone chat this afternoon and interview tomorrow! Good ole Auntie Daph!! Love E.

Email to : enid.p.@setnet.com

From l.purrsey@vsc.net

Subj. Job

Dear Enid. Exc. news. Your Auntie Daph is nodding and cackling in the corner. Not sure I want to know why! Apparently the Matron's an old friend and they did their SRN training together. Love Mum

SIXTH FORM TEXTS

Yaz # to Rosie, Zo, Immi and Sam # Don't forget we're on Interview Duty tomorrow afternoon

Rosie # Great - we'll get to see them all first

Sam # Even better - we'll get to finish the CAKE

Immi # Hope they're not like witchspitz

Yaz # NOBODY cd b as bad as witchspitz

From enid.p.@setnet.com

To l.purrsey@vsc.net **Subj. Job**

I GOT THE JOB!!! Better money! No fares – I can walk there! Gave a month's notice today, I'm owed 3 week's holidays, leave Friday, start Monday! Wow! Will come home for the weekend. Love E.

SIXTH FORM TEXTS

Zo # the only good thing abt that interview afternoon wz the cake

Sam # OMG where did they find that lot!

Rosie # 2 dragonladies 1 mini-witchspitz 1 flower power and a mumsy

Immi # only the Enid one wz ok

Yaz # at least she wznt ancient

From enid.p.@setnet.com

To moggym@topline.com

Subj. BIG NEWS

Hiya. Sorry haven't been in touch. It's all been happenin' here. Guess who's got a new job? Start on Monday! One in the eye for old skinflint-never-do-your-own-work-if-you-can-get-someone-else-to-do-it-for-you Ralph Draisey. Auntie Daph heard about it. Apparently the matron's an old friend from student-nurse days. 'Phone-chat with the headmistress on Tues., interview Wed., gave my notice in Thurs., leave Friday, start on Monday. Howzat! Lazy Draisey's kept me so busy I had 3 weeks' leave owing plus some days in lieu that he wouldn't pay me for, so there we are! The school's near Purrley. St. Catte's Academy. Quite posh with its own grounds. The hall is all wood-panelled. It's very old-fashioned and traditional but I'm to update the office stuff. They've only just got a computer, would you believe! The Head writes absolutely everything in LONGHAND! They call the 6th Years the '6th Form', and the senior classrooms are called 'Formrooms'. Not a bit like our old Saffield Road Comp!!! Am home this weekend so - see you Fri. Whee! Love E

MEMO

TO: Mrs. D. Catford, Housekeeper.

FROM: Tabitha Feline

Ref: Monday's Staff Meeting

Thank you for agreeing to provide coffee and cake for Monday's meeting at 10 a.m. in the staffroom, when I shall be introducing our new P.A./Secretary, Enid Purrsey. Regards. T.

MEMO

TO: All Staff

FROM: Tabitha Feline

Ref: Office Update

Further to the Planning Committee's recommendations and the Governors' agreement that the school admin system is to be modernised. As you are aware, Miss Spitz left us on Friday - to take up a position in the County Archives Office, I believe. Miss Enid Purrsey joins us on Monday as School Secretary and my Personal Assistant, and unfortunately I shall be in London until mid-afternoon. However, I know you will give her a warm welcome, and a helping paw when necessary, until she settles in. The new computer is now installed, as you probably already know.

The Monday Staff Meeting will start at 10.30. At 10 a.m. Mrs. Catford will provide her excellent coffee and cake. I feel an informal get-together for introductions is appropriate. I know you will provide Enid with every assistance. Tabitha Feline

QUICK NOTE to Pawlene McFurley, Deputy Head.

Thanks for undertaking the 'meeting and greeting' function on Monday after the staff meeting. I should be back by mid-afternoon. Do you think it might be a good idea to ask a couple of the Sixth Formers who have free lessons to sit in with Enid for the next day or two, to do repeat introductions and show her around until she's familiar with the layout? I feel that might help her to settle in, even though she had the 'grand tour' when she came for interview last week. See you at dinner. T.

SIXTH FORM TEXTS

Yaz # to **Rosie, Zo, Immi and Sam #** Hv volunteered us for Enid Introduction duty

Sam # who's enid

Rosie # Ms. T's new P.A. doh!

Yaz # we get to use Ms. T's office!!

Immi # wotta thrill

Zo # u can report yr lost key!

Sam # dyou think Mrs. Catfood will do cake?

MEMO

TO: ENID

FROM: Tabitha Feline

Welcome to St. Catte's. As I explained, I am out of school for most of the day. Miss McFurley, our Deputy Head, will be using my office in my absence and so will be on hand to answer any queries. She has arranged for some of the 6th Year students, our Sixth Formers, to be available to help you to find your way around the school and grounds. Take all the time you need to familiarise yourself with the present system set up by Miss Spitz. It is, I fear, a little idiosyncratic.

I append a list of staff. Each has a pigeonhole in the staffroom for messages. Miss Purrkins, our Matron has a telephone. There is another for Mrs. Catford, our Housekeeper, in her office by the kitchen, and one in the Main Hall.

Best wishes,

Tabitha Feline

LIST OF STAFF

- Dr. Tabitha Feline – Head, teaches Language, Number and Classics.
- Ms. Pawlene McFurley – Deputy Head, teaches Life Management.
- Ms. Polly Purrkins - Matron, teaches Health, Hygiene and Being Firm about Food.
- Mrs. Dora Catford - Housekeeper and Cook.
- Ms. Catlin Kittsen - teaches P.E. and Aerial Athletics.
- Miss Furlong - teaches Grooming and Personal Development.
- Miss Mewsing - teaches Music and Drama. Choir Mistress.
- Mlle Minou LaChatte - teaches French.
- Mr. Nepeeta - Caretaker and Gardener.

Email from enid.p@setnet.com

To l.purrsey@vsc.net and moggym@topline.com

Subject. Update

Thought I'd send to you both so only have to type this once! The week's gone really quickly. It's all very new but everyone is so pleasant and it's all so organised and peaceful after Lazy Draisey's rants and sulks. Thank goodness for good ole Auntie Daph and her contacts!! Miss Spitz's system's all cross referenced and is actually easy to follow, but it's all on paper and in folders in filing cabinets. We'll be carrying on using that as Ms. T (that's what everyone calls Dr. Tabitha) knows where everything is but from now on, it'll all go on the computer. Sort of before and after Enid Day. Lol. Aha - some gossip. It seems no-one liked Miss Spitz, who was a bit of a dragon. The kittens called her WitchSpitz!! Apparently there was a big row because she refused to use a computer, and she flounced out. I can't imagine Ms. T having a row - far too dignified. The Deputy Head, Ms. McFurley has drafted in some Sixth Formers, i.e. what we would have called the 6th Years, to help me to get to know everyone and find my way about, which is a huge help. They are great fun. They were allowed to do their work in my office, or Ms. T's (if she wasn't in there) for just a few days while it still seemed all horribly new and confusing, and they're still popping in, which is actually quite useful!

The kitlets (First and Second Years) are adorable, and SO NAUGHTY! Three of them were hanging perilously in the tree outside my window, swaying about like furry little catkins and squeaking alarmingly! I was horrified and hauled them in. They said they were practising their aerial athletics, and looked so sweet and innocent. They scampered off - tails straight up like little pencils, but I did think I heard a muffled giggle. When I told the Sixth Years, they laughed and said that if kitlets look sweet and innocent then they are definitely UP TO SOMETHING, so be VERY suspicious. They are such a nice bunch. Must go to bed. Loadsa lv to all.

SIXTH FORM TEXTS

Immie # to Rosie # Yaz #, Zo #, Sam # Kitlet alert. They were FAR TOO QUIET at break. They've definitely been UP TO SOMETHING but won't say what. KEEP EYES AND EARS OPEN.

LETTER

Letter From Mr. C. Mewslade

CLAWDE A. MEWSLADE, PURRLEY, SURREY

DR. TABITHA FELINE, OBE
St. Catte's Academy.

Dear Dr. Tabitha,

I regret to inform you that when walking alongside the Academy wall this afternoon, I was struck by a flying kitten which fell from the sky like a small furry cannonball. Emitting a series of muffled squeaks, luckily she then managed to slide into the hood of my coat. Extricating her without damage to claws, lining etc. was somewhat tricky, but she emerged unscathed, if slightly dizzy, so I placed her on top of the garden wall and she scampered off. As neither she nor I appeared harmed by this unusual encounter, I judged it best not to ask her name!! I expect it was a game of Kitten Catapult which got out of hand, or indeed - out of paw!!

In NO way is this a complaint. I remember only too clearly the scrapes that my own cat, Lavinia, got herself into when she attended the Academy. Kittens will be kittens! However, I am sure that you will wish to know of this encounter, so you can take steps to prevent your charges leaving the premises in this unorthodox manner, and thus avoid any accidental damage - either to kittens or to unsuspecting passers-by!

I am, dear lady,

Yours sincerely,

Clawde Mewslade

***QUICK NOTE** to Pawlene McFurley, Deputy Head, and Polly Purrkins, Matron.*

The kitlets have surpassed themselves this time! Hurtling over the orchard wall and dropping like furry little conkers! We need to discuss all aspects of this sometime soon. Sherry this evening?

NOTE TO ENID FROM MS. TABITHA

Would you type up the attached Memo and Notice as soon as you can. Thanks.

MEMO : TO ALL STAFF : Please display the following in every Form Room and draw the attention of EACH KITTEN to its contents. I will wish to see the culprits IN MY OFFICE - ASAP. Thanks.

NOTICE: It has come to my attention that kittens (First and Second Years, I suspect), are once again sneaking into the orchard to play Kitten Catapult. THIS MUST STOP. It is dangerous. Passers-by do not expect kittens to drop out of trees on to their heads.

The orchard is OUT OF BOUNDS until further notice. We at St. Catte's are justifiably proud of our achievements in Aerial Athletics and the Extended Leap, but unsupervised training is ABSOLUTELY FORBIDDEN. Signed : Tabitha Feline

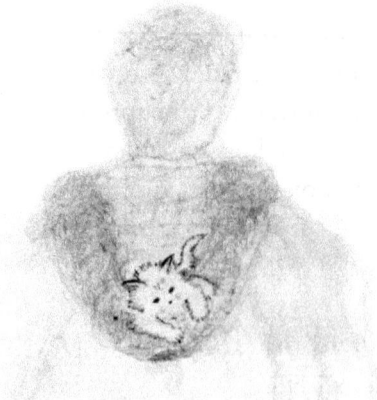

NOTICE BOARD – MAIN HALL

PLEASE NOTE THAT THERE WILL BE NO UNSUPERVISED ACCESS TO THE GARDEN, TENNIS COURTS OR ORCHARD UNTIL FURTHER NOTICE. FIFTH AND SIXTH FORMERS CAN REQUEST PERMISSION ON AN INDIVIDUAL BASIS.

Signed : Tabitha Feline

Email from enid.p@setnet.com **To** l.purrsey@vsc.net **and** moggym@topline.com

Dear all, I asked Ms. McFurley, Deputy Head, about calling classrooms 'form rooms', and 6th Years being 6th 'Formers'. She thinks it goes back centuries, to the first Grammar Schools when there was just one schoolroom and one schoolmaster. Each year group sat in a row on the same bench, called a 'form', so 'form 1' was for the 1st Years, Year 2 sat on 'form' 2, and so on. The schoolroom, where all the benches/ forms were was called the 'formroom', so 'Form' came to mean class or year-group. So now we know! Logical, I suppose, in a quaint, old-fashioned way. Like Ms. Spitz's filing system lol. Love E.

MEMO : TO MS. CATLIN KITTSEN FROM TABITHA FELINE

I'd be glad if you could put on your thinking cap about the latest incidents of Kitten Catapult. I'm amazed they managed to propel themselves so far! Perhaps you could join me for coffee with any ideas you might have? Enid knows when I'm free. Thanks.

Tabitha Feline

SIXTH FORM TEXTS:

Yaz # to Rosie # Sam # Immi # Zo # Hooray. The kitlets are PRIS-ONERS, they're not allowed out

Sam # OMG they'll go stir crazy

Zo # prob start banister swinging again

Rosie # they won't dare to

Immi # they're in too much trouble already

LETTER TO MR. A. MEWSLADE FROM DR. TABITHA FELINE

Dear Mr. Mewslade,

Thank you for your letter. It was very kind of you to take such a tolerant view of the occurrence yesterday afternoon. Not many people, even those associated with the Academy, would have been quite so unperturbed by a kitten bombardment. Yes, I do remember incidents when Lavinia was a pupil - particularly clear is the frog affair! As you say, kittens will be kittens, but by the same token, rules are also rules. The kittens in question will be severely reprimanded.

I hope you and Lavinia are both well, and look forward to seeing you at the Open Day and Literary Festival.

Yours sincerely,

Tabitha Feline

NOTICE BOARD – MAIN HALL

PLEASE NOTE THAT THE LIBRARY HAS BEEN BOOKED FOR A GOVERNORS' MEETING AT 6.30 THIS EVENING

SIXTH FORM TEXTS:

Sam # to Immi # Rosie # Yaz # Zo # : Told Mrs. Catfood we'd serve the coffee at the Governors' meeting. Sooo we get to finish the cake afterwards. Lurve Catfood's cake

Email from enid.p@setnet.com **To** l.purrsey@vsc.net and moggym@topline.com

Loads going on: CAT-ASTROPHE, you could say lol. Kitlets in really BIG TROUBLE, there's extra meetings and lots to do but I'm actually enjoying it all. Ms. T is still writing things by hand, but is now passing the office stuff to me! PROGRESS! Am fine. More next time. Love E. Xx

P.S.By the way - kitlets are 1st and 2nd years, kits are 3rd and 4th years, Kitcats are the older ones but usually just called 5th or 6th Formers, but kittens covers them all really. In case you were wondering ! I'm just about getting used to it!!!! Xxxx

NOTE TO ENID FROM MS. TABITHA :

As the Governors have given permission for us to start alterations to the orchard and tennis court area, would you arrange for us to have quotations from local landscaping/gardening firms. You'll find the people we've used before in Ms. Spitz's system somewhere, I'm sure. Thanks.

LETTER TO CHAIRMAN OF THE GOVERNORS.

Dear Ms. Catwallader,

Thank you for your support in the matter of the re-structuring of part of the gardens to create an outdoor training area for athletics.

As you commented, Catlin Kittsen's presentation was impressive, and as a Bronze Medallist in the recent Olympuss Games, we can rely on her professional expertise.

Yours sincerely,

Tabitha Feline

MEMO TO MS. TABITHA FROM CATLIN KITTSEN

With reference to the Kitten Catapult prevention scheme, as requested I have prepared a handout about the construction of a training area for Aerial Athletics and the Extended Leap, to be distributed with the agenda for the staff meeting. I have given a brief outline of the removal of some of the trees adjacent to the garden walls, alteration to the present tennis courts, access from the gymnasium and possible timetabling.

As some of the 1st and 2nd Year kitlets are very keen and unusually talented, I feel sure that if we channel their enthusiasm into legitimate training activities, we might be able to create a team at competition level. Some of the Third and Fourth Years have also expressed an interest.

Catlin Kittsen

SIXTH FORM TEXTS:

Immie # the tennis courts are bein dug up

Zo # no one ever plays anyway

Immie # Catty Kittsen's startin a leapin' Olympuss athletics team

Sam # we don't have to train do we

Yaz # I hate athletics

Sam # I hate everything

Yaz # TOLD u not to stuff yourself with that cake

Zo # it's mostly training for 1st n 2nd years

Immie # good. Keep 'em out of trouble

Rosie # Tire the little beggars out!

Zo # they're not really goin to be called the St. Catte's Catapults are they|?

Sam # wot?

Immie # wot?

Yaz # wot?

Rosie # wot??

LETTER : from MS. TRISTIA W. SPITZ - delivered BY HAND.

TRISTIA W. SPITZ

Dr. Tabitha Feline,

St. Catte's Academy.

Dear Dr. Tabitha,

It has come to my attention from two reliable sources that kittens are dropping from the orchard trees on to the heads of startled passers-by. This is not only dangerous but would be an extremely unsettling experience for anybody, particularly for the aged or infirm, and, of course, raises impawtant Health and Safety issues.

That kittens are able to leave your premises in this dangerous manner and without your knowledge is a serious breach of care. This is so obviously a disciplinary matter that I felt I had to bring it to your attention immediately. It is not what is expected from St. Catte's.

I trust you are well.

Yours sincerely,

Tristia W. Spitz

QUICK NOTE : FROM Ms. Tabitha to Pawlene McFurley, Deputy Head, and Polly Purrkins, Matron:

I have received a missive from Miss Spitz accusing us of 'a breach of care'!! Sherry this evening to discuss? T.

Email to l.purrsey@vsc.net **and** moggym@topline.com **from** enid.p@setnet.com

Hiya Mum, Dad, Auntie Daph and Mogs: There's been loads happening here! Remember I told you about those naughty kittens in the tree? Well they sneaked into the orchard to play Kitten Catapult (they bounce on branches then see how far they can leap) and one of them hurtled over the wall like a fluffy rocket, hit someone and slid down into the hood of his anorak! Talk about a shock – who'd expect to be hit by a flying kitten!!! But he carefully fished the kitlet out of his hood and shoved her back over the wall. Anyway, he was OK about it - apparently his kitten had been at St. Catte's and was a real tearaway for a while - got told off by Miss Spitz and put frogs in her desk drawer to get even! You wonder how she dared! He wrote to Ms. T just to let her know. But Miss Spitz heard gossip and wrote virtually accusing Ms. T of negligence! No wonder the kits call her WitchSpitz! There was uproar here for a while - extra Governors' meeting and all sorts going on and now Ms. Kittsen (PE. Won a bronze at the Olympuss!) is forming competition teams. Some of the kits are really talented and she's got them puffing about doing press-ups and training. The 6th formers are delighted – tire the little beggars out, they say! The tennis courts will be changed into a big training area and guess what – the trees by the orchard wall are being removed so there won't be any more airborne little athletes going AWOL! Lol. See you at the weekend. Love E.

P.S. WitchSpitz came in to deliver a letter to Ms. T. Obviously dying to know what's going on. Nosey ole batcat! Will tell all on Friday XX

LETTER TO MISS SPITZ FROM DR. TABITHA FELINE:

Dear Miss Spitz,

Thank you for your letter. We would indeed be in 'breach of care' if St. Catte's kittens were allowed to leave the premises without our knowledge. However, this is not the case. I feel your informants may have been referring to alterations which are taking place in the grounds. Some of our kittens are extremely talented and with Ms. Kittsen's skilled coaching in Aerial Athletics and the Extended Leap, have increased their range beyond the present facilities. This was pointed out to us by the parent of one of our ex-pupils and we are now in the process of installing upgraded training facilities, utilising trees considered to be too close to the orchard wall. Nevertheless, I was interested to hear how far rumour can stray from the truth. Ms. Kitttsen, as you know, is an Olympuss Bronze medallist and has the complete support of the Governors.

No doubt you yourself will be interested in seeing the new developments at our Literary Festival and Open Day

Yours sincerely,

Tabitha Feline

SIXTH FORM TEXTS :

Rosie # guess who complained about kittens dropping out of trees on to people's heads

Sam # who else.. witchspitz

Immi # boo hiss

Zo # she's the pits

Yaz # sneaky snitch

Immi # wotta bitch

Rosie # glad she quit

Immi # coo we're poets

Yaz # bit more work n it can go into the Poetry Competition ROFL!

Email : to l.purrsey@vsc.net **and** moggym@topline.com **from** enid.p@setnet.com

Dear Mum, Dad and everyone. Thought I'd have a quiet day today as Ms. T's in London but we've got a crisis. Kitten stuck up a tree. OMG!!! Chaos here at the moment. Will keep you posted. Love E

SIXTH FORM TEXTS :

Zo # its Sofronia stuck up the tree

Sam # pluckin ell! she hates heights

Rosie # nobody tell witchspitz

Immi # or she'll be sticking her oar in again

Yaz # you mean stickin her paw in lol.

Email : to enid.p@setnet.com **from** l.purrsey@vsc.net

ENID WOULD YOU PLEASE BRING US UP TO DATE ON THE KITTEN-STUCK-UP-THE-TREE SAGA. We're dying of suspense here. Tried to text and ring. HAVE YOU CHARGED YOUR PHONE? Love Mum

Email : to l.purrsey@vsc.net **and** moggym@topline.com **from** enid.p@setnet.com

Hi Mum, Dad, Auntie Daph, Mogs and everyone. Sorry. Was home late. Had to finish some work for Ms. T to take with her to a meeting in London. Yes. Huge drama. Kitlet stuck up tree, piteous meowlings, Mamselle La Chatte hysterical and phoning the Fire Brigade and having to be forcibly restrained by Matron and Catlin Kittsen, and Mr. Nepeta to the rescue with his trusty extension ladder. Phew! Pawd knows what she was doing up there. He had to prise her off as she was hanging on to her branch for dear life, then she attached herself to his jacket and clung on as he climbed down. They couldn't unhook her from the jacket so he took it off and Matron wrapped her up in it and cuddled her until she opened her eyes and unclenched her claws. She's really sweet – white and fluffy with blue eyes. Never a dull moment!!! Hope to be home Friday. Love E.

Email : from st.catte's@set.net.com **to DR. TABITHA FELINE from Pawlene McFurley, Deputy Head**

Just to set your mind at rest. We extracted Sofronia from the tree without having to call the Fire Brigade. Mr. Nepeta did sterling service with his extending ladder. Sofronia was clinging to the branch like a fluffy limpet and there was a nasty moment as he was trying to prise her off when they were both swaying perilously, but she buried her claws into his jacket. If it hadn't been padded and she'd buried her claws in him—twenty needle-like little claws! The mind boggles!! She was so inextricably hooked to the jacket it was impossible to disentangle her, so Mr. N. took it off and Matron wrapped her up in it and soothed her until her eyes opened and she started squeaking. She actually looked like a baby kangaroo - a Joey, I believe they are called. Matron is keeping an eye on her for the night, we are all breathing a sigh of relief, and Mr. Nepeta is being fed right royally by Mrs. Catford. I'm afraid his jacket is rather the worse for wear. See you on your return. P.

MEMO: TO MATRON FROM CATLIN KITSEN

As we discussed this afternoon, I've jotted down the background to my concerns about Sofronia for your info before you see her this afternoon. She is quiet and slightly timid, and has no problem with the normal PE programme, but recently has been making excuses for not doing Aerial Training. Her floor exercises are entirely up to standard. Since her rescue by Mr. Nepeta, she is reluctant to do anything which involves more than two paws off the ground at the same time. Understandable of course, as she was so terrified by that experience. Obviously all kitlets have to do the same work, but the others are part of the aerial training team, have no problem with heights and so feel superior. They are rather inclined to giggle about the tree incident, which of course, makes it worse for Sofronia. If you will check her over to make sure she's OK, I'm sure we can come up with a solution. Thanks. Catlin

MEMO: TO MS. TABITHA FELINE FROM POLLY PURRKINS, MATRON

I have seen Sofronia and checked her over. Physically, she's fine. A sensitive kitlet with a vivid imagination and a real fear of heights which is why Mr. Nepeta had such difficulty unclamping her from the branch - and his jacket. She now regards him as a hero, by the way and has written him a thank-you. In verse! The copy she gave me is attached. Catlin sees her as a challenge and is devising a personal training programme. Regards, P

THANK YOU POEM from Sofronia to Mr. Nepeta :

I was stuck in a tree

And you rescued me.

Thank you Mr. Nepeta

You're a world beater. From Sofronia.

Email : to l.purrsey@vsc.net **and** moggym@topline.com **from** enid.p@setnet.com

Hiya Mum, Dad, Auntie Daph and Mogs. Still as busy. There are so many memos flying around at the moment. Did I say that Ms. T's a complete communications NUT. Everything has to be in writing with a copy in the file. Her favourite motto is 'Good organisation needs excellent communication'! She still writes everything by hand anyway, so I just file her stuff in Miss Spitz's loony system, and give Ms. T print-outs of emails etc. so it's not double the work. Apparently my system is very different from Miss Spitz's. Who'd have thought!! According to the Sixth Formers , she used to guard the pencils and stationery like gold and LISTENED IN on everyone's phone conversations, and insisted that the registers were handed in at the end of each month totalled accurately, and then she checked THEM ALL and returned them to the staff if she found errors! Blimey. Guess who won't be doing that if I can help it!! That's what computers are for! Tell Auntie Daph that Matron sends her regards. Loadsa love. E.

MEMO : TO MS. TABITHA FELINE FROM POLLY PURRKINS, MATRON.

The kitlets are so tired with all Catlin's training activities that they fall asleep as soon as they are put to bed in what they are calling a 'kitten cuddle' all squashed in a heap in one bed. They are certainly sleeping soundly, so I would suggest we use a communal basket for those who prefer to cuddle in a huddle to sleep and the basket bedding will be laundered weekly as usual, of course. Some individual beds won't be used, which should produce a saving on laundry bills and give Mrs. Catford's staff more time for other duties. I'm sure you'll have no objection to us trying this out, if this is what the kits prefer. They do actually look very sweet...when they're sleeping!

The Third and Fourth Years are giving cause for concern. Recently they have been drowsy and lethargic in their form-room during the day and far too lively for comfort at 'lights out'. I suspect some of them might even have been 'banister swinging', and I have warned the Sixth Form duty-supervisors to be on their guard.

Just one other point. The Lost Property cupboard is absolutely full, and there is a swooningly strong whiff of catnip in my office from all the toys which have been left around the place and ended up there. A collection-day soon, I think! Regards. P.

NOTE TO ENID FROM MS. TABITHA :

Could you type the attached, put up the notice and let the staff have the memo sometime this morning. Thanks.

MEMO: TO ALL STAFF FROM MS. TABITHA FELINE, HEAD

There is far too much in the Lost Property cupboard. Please take each class down in turn to identify and claim lost items, particularly those containing catnip. There are so many catnip toys that Matron is becoming quite woozy in her office next door! Anything left after Friday will be delivered to the Royal Society for the Prevention of Cruelty to Cats' Charity shop with any other donations to the R.S.P.C.C. which kittens care to make.

Would you also remind kittens of the rules for the use of the Main Staircase.

Tabitha Feline

NOTICE BOARD – MAIN HALL

THE MAIN STAIRCASE IS A UNIQUE FEATURE OF OUR ACADEMY AND WE ARE JUSTLY PROUD OF ITS ELEGANCE. PLEASE REMEMBER TO OBEY THE STAIRCASE RULES : SINGLE FILE AND NO RUNNING.

LEANING OR SWINGING ON THE BANISTERS IS STRICTLY PROHIBITED.

Signed: Tabitha Feline

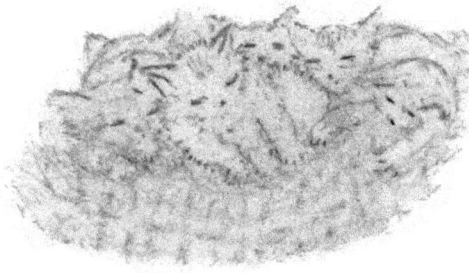

MEMO: TO MS. TABITHA FELINE, HEAD, AND MS. PURRKINS, MATRON, FROM CATLIN KITTSEN

Sofronia is responding well. We have drawn up an individual training programme, having first ascertained what she can now accomplish easily, and she will chart her progress session by session. Heights are still presenting a problem for her, but the aim is that she will be able to jump from a chair to a table to a windowsill by the end of the term.

She will be involved with the Aerial Athletics and Extended Leap team as their official Scorer, will attend all training sessions and competitions and will keep the records of their individual achievements, so her excellent number skills are utilised and she is now an acknowledged member of the team. She is making really good progress.

I have encouraged her to write about her fears and she will, of course, continue with her twice weekly chats with Matron.

Catlin Kittsen

MEMO : TO MS. CATLIN KITTSEN FROM MS. TABITHA FELINE

Thank you for your memo about Sofronia. She is obviously responding well to the individual programme you have devised for her. The topic of our class today was 'Conveying Emotion and the Silent Miaow', and I am sure you will be interested in what Sofronia wrote. It does give us a clear indication of how she feels, and I absolutely agree that it will help if she can put her emotions into words. I have suggested to her that she enters her poem into our Literary Festival Poetry Competition. Regards,

Tabitha Feline

Sofronia's Poem

Being high in the air

Gives me a scare, and

I'm shaking with fear and fright.

With a butterfly tum

I could do with a chum

34

To help me in my plight.

I feel left in the lurch

On a perilous perch

And I'm hanging on ever so tight.

It isn't much fun,

So PLEASE someone come.

I don't want to be here all night.

SIXTH FORM TEXTS :

Zo # to Rosie #, Yaz #, Immi #, Sam #: Wot the ell wz up with the 3rd n 4th formers tonight. Pandemonium!! I've seen matron about their behaviour n she wants to discuss it with us. C u in her office asap. Wot's got into them now?

QUICK NOTE : FROM Ms. Tabitha to Polly Purrkins, Matron, and Pawlene McFurley, Deputy Head :

We'll need to get to the bottom of whatever was going on tonight with the 3rd and 4th Years. Over-giggly, over-excited, out of control and out of their dormitory. Sherry? T.

NOTICE BOARD – MAIN HALL

AS YOU KNOW – CLAW SHARPENING ON BANISTERS OR FURNITURE IS NOT ALLOWED.

PLEASE USE THE SCRATCHING POSTS SITUATED IN THE CORRIDOR OUTSIDE THE GYMNASIUM AND ON THE PLAYGROUND PERIMETER.

Signed: Tabitha Feline

SIXTH FORM TEXTS :

Rosie # Matron says we've got to meet her and Ms. McFurley

Yaz # there were deffo wet pawprints

Immi # and the window wz deffo open

Sam # they wouldn't be climbing out WOULD THEY???

Zo # dunno but somethings going on

Yaz # all that squeaky giggling

Rosie # pawd knows wot they're up to now

ENTRY: LOGGED INTO INCIDENT BOOK BY MS. P. McFURLEY, DEPUTY HEAD

Repawted to Matron by Duty Sixth Form Supervisors.

The Sixth Form Supervisors had reason for concern and repawted to Matron who asked me to attend. There was an open window on the first-floor landing outside the dormitories and wet pawprints. It seems pawsible that a kitten has climbed out and back again. Impawsible to ascertain which one: nobody would admit it and all were damp – freshly washed and ready for bed, but far too sweet and innocent for comfort with big eyes and groomed whiskers and a general air of suppressed giddiness which really gives me pawse for thought.

I have asked the staff to organise extra observation, and frequent patrols on all landings have been put in place.

Mrs. Catford is inspecting all her supplies in case additives could be responsible, and has suggested that she should serve only the very plainest food for the moment, but we feel this is unlikely to be the cause as the 1st and 2nd Years do not seem to be involved. They are eating well and are sleeping particularly well with their kitten cuddle basket arrangement, thanks to Ms. Kittsen's AA + EL training.

Signed : **Pawlene McFurley**

NOTE : TO ENID FROM TABITHA FELINE :

Enid: Would you make a list of the main topic headings for each subject. You will find these in the 'Curriculum' file, under the heading 'Teaching Programmes'. We'll need them before the Open Day Planning Meeting. Thanks.

PLANNING COMMITTEE MEETING : LITERARY FESTIVAL AND OPEN DAY PROGRAMME

DISPLAYS AND DEMONSTRATIONS : MAIN CURRICULUM TOPIC AREAS:

<u>Personal Development</u> : Cuteness, Grooming and Fur-ball Management, the Silent Miaow, Choosing your Human and/or Home: adoration factor, comfort, location etc.

<u>Manipulation and Management of Humans</u>: Looking Reproachful, the Disapproving Tail-tip Flip, the Turning of the Back in Disapproval, the use of Quiet Dignity, Refusing the Cuddle, etc.

<u>Being Firm about Food</u> : Never eating anything which hasn't come off your Human's plate, or out of a freshly opened sachet/packet/tin unless you caught it yourself. The importance of the 'Sniff Tentatively, Look Reproachful and Walk Away Rapidly' technique etc.

<u>Aerial Athletics and Extended Leap (AA+EL) Team Demo</u> plus crikcat, pawball, gymcastics, tossing the mouse, stair ping-pong, curtain climbing techniques, etc.

<u>Music</u> : performance by the choir 'The St. Catte's Chorus'

<u>Drama</u> : Titles to be decided – suggestions ?

<u>French</u> : Poise, Posing, Photogenics and "The Attitude/Depawtment 'Exotique'"

MEMO : TO ALL STAFF FROM TABITHA FELINE :

<u>**PLANNING MEETING**</u>

<u>Literary Festival and Open Day Preparation.</u>

A list of the broad topic areas for each subject is attached. Would you start giving some thought to suitable choices for the above, prior to the Planning

Meeting next week. We can then discuss which activities are feasible for the kittens to demonstrate, and start preparations.

All ideas will be welcome. At this stage, of course, we only need to concentrate upon a broad outline. We can look at the details later. I will send round a suggested list of titles for the drama performances in the near future.

Tabitha Feline

QUICK NOTE : FROM CATLIN KITSEN TO MATRON :

For your info. before Sofronia's session with you. She was extremely upset this morning – all quivery whiskers and quiet, so obviously something is very wrong. I'm teaching all day so won't be able to follow this through. It has something to do with the 3rd and 4th Years laughing at Mr. Nepeta, who is still her hero, for not weeding the gardens properly. Hopefully she will tell you what's going on. Catlin

QUICK NOTE : TO ENID FROM MATRON :

ENID : REALLY URGENT. Need a meeting with Ms. T and Ms. McFurley A.S.A.P. and could you get hold of Mr. Nepeta for me JUST AS SOON AS POSS. Thanks.

QUICK NOTE : FROM MATRON TO CATLIN KITTSEN

Sofronia is fine but we could have a problem. Could you see me JUST AS SOON AS POSS. Urgent!!!

QUICK NOTE : FROM ENID TO MRS. CATFORD :

URGENT - Tried to ring you – could you ask Mr. Nepeta to contact Matron URGENTLY as soon as he comes in for his coffee. Thanks. Enid

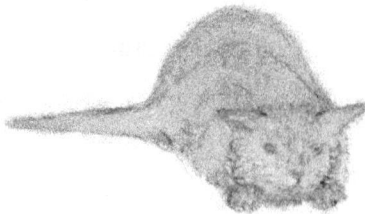

SIXTH FORM TEXTS :

Rosie # has matron taken up gardening

Sam # Wot?

Rosie # she's in the flower bed with Mr. Nepeta

Yaz # wot?

Zo # wot?

Immi # perhaps there's a thing

Zo # wot thing

Immi # a fling

Sam # THAT IS NOT AN IMAGE I WANT IN MY HEAD

Yaz # eeew the stuff of nightmares

Rosie # why are they digging in the flower beds

Immi # deffo time for a recce see you outside in purrsuit of gossip..!

QUICK NOTE : to ENID FROM MS. TABITHA :

ENID: URGENT: would you type this and DELIVER to staff ASAP. I'm afraid you'll have to interrupt classes if they're teaching.

MEMO : TO ALL STAFF FROM TABITHA FELINE - TO BE DELIV-ERED TO EACH CLASSROOM BY HAND.

There will be a brief meeting in the Staffroom as soon as classes finish for lunch.

Tabitha Feline

NOTICE

GARDENS AND GROUNDS
ARE OUT OF BOUNDS
TO ALL KITTENS

Signed: Tabitha Feline

Email : to l.purrsey@vsc.net from enid.p@setnet.com

Sorry I missed your call. Was out of the office - had to take urgent notes around to Mrs. Catford and all the teachers. There's a bit of a mystery going on and everything's upside down. Mrs. T. Is in the garden with Mr. Nepeta and none of the kittens are allowed out. Speak to you soon. Love E. XX

MEMO : TO MR. NEPETA FROM MS. TABITHA FELINE

Thank you for your suggestions this morning. If I have remembered it correctly, you intend to rearrange the border planting roughly as follows:

Remove the catmint hedge from beneath the classroom windows in case it is contributing to the lethargy apparent in the kittens in the afternoons.

Replace with 'stimulating' plants. I think you mentioned basil, mint, jasmine, rose and rosemary. The final choice is yours, of course.

Replant all the catmint underneath the dormitory windows, in the hope that it proves calming and relaxing. I think you also mentioned lavender and possibly valerian here, but again, I leave the choice to you.

We are all completely at a loss to explain where the 'weed' which was flourishing in the herbaceous border actually came from. It is indeed a mystery, as is the fact that the kittens found it. I hope this extra and unexpected work will not cause too much pressure. Thank you again for all your help.

Tabitha Feline

SIXTH FORM TEXTS :

Immi # wot is going on

Zo # it's still the 3rd/4th year thing

Yaz # Sofronia says they've been eating grass

Sam # but we ALL eat grass

Rosie # not with weed in it!

Immi # wot?

Zo # wot?

Yaz # wot?

Sam # wot?

Immi # wot you mean WEED weed

Rosie # that's why we're all on extra bedtime duties for the next few nights -

to quell the kits. Staff as well!

QUICK NOTE TO PAWLENE McFURLEY DEPUTY HEAD, AND POLLY PURRKINS, MATRON FROM TABITHA FELINE:

As we shall all be involved in extra supervision after 'lights out' for the time being, how about popping in for a sherry after we've finished. T.

41

SIXTH FORM TEXTS :

Yaz # how did it get in the border?

Immi # HOW DID THEY KNOW IT WZ THERE

Zo # bird dropped a seed?

Sam # bet those little beggars PLANTED it

Rosie # bet witchspitz planted it

Immi # so she could shop us

Sam # OMG a raid by the Drug Squad

Rosie # cue hysterics from Mamselle

Yaz # aha SHE might have planted it

Zo # nah bet it wz witchspit

Email : to l.purrsey@vsc.net **and** moggym@topline.com **from** enid.p@setnet.com

Dear Mum, Dad, Auntie Daph and Mogs and everyone. Phew! It's been quite a week. I'll try to condense it or I'll be here all night. Right. 3rd and 4th years over-lively, playing up at night and falling asleep during the day. Sofronia (kitten up tree, rescued by Mr. Nepeta who is now her hero) hears them making fun of him, is upset and happens to mention to Matron that that wasn't fair just because the lawn has weeds in it and they ate weeds with their grass, as gardens always have weeds and grass. Grass! Weed! Alarm bells ping in Matron's head. Light-bulb moment!! Garden is closely scrutinised and STRANGE FRONDY PLANT is subsequently discovered!! Which THE KITS HAVE BEEN EATING!! No huge commotion, all calm on the surface but massive investigation commences. All kittens kept in, lots of questioning of the culprits, big consultations - and extensive garden alterations now in hand, borders being dug up and moved. Plants are being chosen to liven 'em up by day and soothe 'em by night! AND NO WEED! Er - only the usual nettles and dandelions and things!!

All sorts of extra supervision going on, Matron's doing extra Health and Hygiene sessions, Catlin Kittsen (she's really nice, by the way), is doing the 'healthy mind in the healthy body' stuff and extra PE and training, Ms. Mewley (music and drama) has scheduled in extra choir rehearsals to keep them occupied and Mamselle is being hysterically dramatic (or dramatically hysterical!), as usual. The sixth form swear Witchspitz planted it before she left so she could have us raided by the Drug Squad! They are hilarious! Wotta muddle. Would be really funny if it wasn't so serious. Kittens as high as kites at St. Catte's. Whatever next? Ms. T is remarkably calm and organised about it all, of course - you never see her get her whiskers in a twist, and they all really do work together as a team.

Better get to bed. Home at weekend. Love to all. E

NOTICE

WILL THE KITTENS WHO KILLED THE FEATHER DUSTER IN THE BACK HALL KINDLY CLEAR UP THE MESS.

PLEASE NOTE – CHASING THE FEATHERS AROUND DOES NOT CONSTITUTE CLEARING UP. I SHALL BE CHECKING THE AREA VERY SHORTLY.

Signed : Tabitha Feline

NOTE TO ENID FROM TABITHA FELINE:

List of titles attached. Would you type them up and attach to the Agenda for the Planning Meeting. Thanks.

PLANNING COMMITTEE MEETING

LITERARY FESTIVAL AND OPEN DAY

Suggested Drama Titles for consideration :

Shakespeare : The Tempuss, King Ear, Troilus and Pussida, A Winter's Tail, Titus Andronipuss,

A Midsummer Fright's Scream (Sixth Form's suggestion).

Dickens : A Tail of Two Kitties

I look forward to hearing your ideas and comments

Tabitha Feline

NOTE : TO MATRON FROM MRS. CATFORD:

Polly : I think I need to spray the dormitories: it may be over-cautious but better safe than sorry!

Dora

SIXTH FORM TEXT :

Immi # OMG! OMG! OMG! Saw ole Catfood with the fleaspray..! NIT ALERT !!!!!!!!

LETTER FROM MISS TRISTIA W. SPITZ TO DR. TABITHA FELINE

TRISTIA W. SPITZ

Dr. Tabitha Feline, Principuss,

St. Catte's Academy.

Dear Dr. Tabitha,

It gives me great pleasure to accept your invitation to the St. Catte's Literary Festival and Open Day. I shall be interested to see the new aromatic garden I hear you have planted.

As I am something of an expert in this field, I shall be pleased to offer help and advice. Please let me know when it would be convenient to call.

Kind regards,

Yours sincerely,

Tristia W. Spitz

LETTER FROM DR. TABITHA FELINE TO MISS TRISTIA W. SPITZ

Dear Miss Spitz,

Thank you for your letter. I'm afraid we cannot claim anything as grand as an aromatic garden. Merely moving the catmint does not quite place us in that category, although we have also planted some lavender, as you will, I am sure, see on Open Day.

I hope you are well.

Yours sincerely,

Tabitha Feline

QUICK NOTE FROM DR. TABITHA TO PAWLENE McFURLEY, DEPUTY HEAD AND POLLY PERKINS, MATRON.

Miss Spitz has decided that my polite mention of Open Day constitutes a personal invitation to attend! She also informs me that we have a 'new aromaticc garden'. Where DOES she get this garbled information from!! Sherry? T.

SIXTH FORM TEXTS :

Rosie # witchspitz is saying we've got an aromatic garden

Sam # have we. Where

Immi # how would SHE know

Yaz # bet she's been spying.

Zo # prob binoculars over the wall

Sam # bugged the begonias!

Yaz # camera in the camellias!!

Immi # checking for WEED

Rosie # ha ha

Zo # plantin it, more like lol

NOTE : TO ENID FROM POLLY PERKINS, MATRON

Would you contact the Medical Centre and arrange a date for the kittens' routine medical check-ups and any booster jabs which may be required. Tell them to leave all the organisation to us. Thanks.

MEMO : TO MATRON FROM ENID, c.c. MS. TABITHA

Mr. Catterie and his team from the Medical Centre have confirmed that they will be here next Wednesday afternoon. He said that this time he would be very pleased indeed to leave ALL the organisation of the session entirely in your hands!

SIXTH FORM TEXTS :

Zo # watch out Matron's on the prowl

Rosie # she's doing random fur checks

Immi # norah the nitnurse rides again!!

Yaz # brandishing her trusty toothcomb

Sam # I hate the feel of the stuff they put on the back of my neck

Zo # disgustin greasy drops

Rosie # better than havin fleas and all that scratchin

MEMO: TO ALL STAFF FROM TABITHA FELINE

ROUTINE MEDICAL CHECK-UPS

As you probably know, Mr. Catterie will be here on Wednesday next. I am sure that the debacle last time will be etched upon your memory, when the smallest kitlets, hopelessly confused by the whole process, kept joining and rejoining the queues and were in imminent danger of being inoculated and flea-treated over and over again. Of course, Miss Spitz WAS only trying to help when she started marking them as they came out, but she was rather over-enthusiastic with the poster paint. It was inevitable that after the play-time pouncing games they ALL ended up paint-bespattered, even the older kittens who were trying to keep order, which only added to the general chaos. Not our finest hour, I'm afraid. This time, we will ourselves timetable the whole process from start to finish. Mr. Catterie says he is more than pleased to relinquish any responsibility for organisation, and Matron will again take the opportunity to administer flea-treatment as the kittens file past. Your suggestions as to how we arrange the session will be welcome.

Tabitha Feline

SIXTH FORM TEXTS :

Yaz # next Wednesday's D day

Immi # u mean FLEA DAY lol

Rosie # we're on duty, dunno details yet

Sam # well it can't be as bad as last time

Zo # most of that wz witchspitz'z fault, she kept interferin n giving orders

Sam # took ages to get that paint off

Yaz # SHE wz covered in it as well ha ha

Immi # served her right

Zo # looked a complete idiot

Immi # trying to keep order

Yaz # covered in paint

Rosie # and BLOWIN A WHISTLE

Sam # wot self respectin' kitten wd EVER answer to a WHISTLE lol!

Zo # especially blown by witchspitz!!!

MEMO : FROM TABITHA FELINE TO ALL STAFF

MEDICAL CHECK-UP SESSION

Thank you for your prompt response and ideas. The biggest problem is of course, preventing the kittens from washing each other before the flea treatment dries. I particularly like the idea of tying a bow on each of them, which will certainly keep the little ones occupied and we can see at a glance who has been done. Enid has already ordered the ribbons locally and will collect them tomorrow.

Tabitha Feline

Email : to l.purrsey@vsc.net **and** moggym@topline.com **from** enid.p@setnet.com

Dear Mum, Dad, Auntie Daph and Mogs. How's things. All's well here and I'm really enjoying this job. Everyone is so nice and there's always so much going on. At the moment it's preparation for the kits' medical check-ups, Mrs. Catford is in the middle of her flea-prevention programme and Matron will be applying/administering the drops when the kittens have been checked by Mr. Catterie, the school's medical adviser (we don't actually call him 'the vet'). Apparently last time the medical team was here, they insisted on organising the session themselves, but had no idea of the kittens' talent for creating mayhem, and WitchSpitz took it upon herself to 'help', which made the chaos infinitely worse. This time it's been decided that the Sixth Form are going to tie a bow on each kitten once they're done. Cute! When I went to collect the ribbons, WitchSpitz appeared as if by magic at my elbow, saw the big bag of ribbons and the nosey ole batcat wanted to know what it was for! Then she said that I had bought more than enough to dress a Maypole and she knew all about THAT because she used to organise Maypole Dancing classes, so I just smiled and beat a hasty retreat. Then Mr. Nepeta told Mrs. Catford that WitchSpitz is going around town telling everyone that the kittens are going to do an Old English Maypole Dance on Open Day!!! Can you imagine it? They'd end up strangling themselves and tangling the audience up as well!!!! See you Friday. Love E.

MEMO: TO ALL STAFF FROM TABITHA FELINE

MEDICAL CHECK-UP SESSION

As agreed during discussion this afternoon, the programme will run as follows :

Classes will take place as usual.

Matron will send a Sixth Former to tell Tutors when to bring their class down.

Each kitten will see Mr. Catterie and then Matron, one at a time.

Sixth Formers will tie a ribbon on the kittens as each emerges.

Kittens will then have a supervised play-session outdoors, unless it is raining.

Mrs. Catford is going to arrange refreshments for Mr. Catterie and his team.

Dinner will be served at the usual time.

Tabitha Feline

SIXTH FORM TEXT :

Sam # to Immi #, Rosie #, Yaz #, Zo # : Have volunteered us all to help Mrs Catfood with the refreshments. Yay! CAKE!!!!

Email : to l.purrsey@vsc.net **and** moggym@topline.com **from** enid.p@setnet.com

Phew! Well, this has been a very funny day - funny peculiar as well as funny ha ha!! All the kits have had their medical check-ups and flea-treatments. Everything was very organised, each class came down and waited quietly with their tutors, each kitten was seen by Mr. Catterie and Matron, then the Sixth Formers tied a bow on them and they went out to play. The ribbons gave them something to think about other than washing off the flea stuff. The Sixth Formers had tied their own bows on their paws and looked very elegant as they supervised the kits and helped to serve the coffee and Mrs. Catford's cake. The younger ones spent ages chewing at their own ribbons and leaping on each other's to get them off, so looked really funny and cute rolling about all over the place. The 3rd and 4th Years were a RIOT ! They scratched and scrabbled and jumped on each other's to untie them, and tied them on trees and swung on them and were really amewsing to watch. Some of them tied the ribbons on their tails, then ran around squeaking while the others chased them and tried to pounce. One little 1st Year got it caught on a back claw and chased it round and round until she was so tired she fell asleep and had to be carried off and put to bed! One or two swung them round and round their heads doing 'twirlies'. Then to our complete astonishment, M'selle hurtled in with a massively long length of ribbon and leaped and whirled and swirled and swooped about dancing an energetic and exotic sort of wild fandango !!! Goodness!!! Who would have thought. Nobody expected THAT! The kits were VERY impressed. Everyone else was utterly astounded! I'm not sure I've quite recovered even yet! I don't think I'll ever be able to see Mamselle in quite the same way ever again!

The ribbons were really clever psychology - the kits were far too busy with them to try and wash the flea-drops off even before M'selle appeared - and by the time her floorshow had finished, they'd probably forgotten all about them! Coo - never a dull moment!! Hope all's well with you all. Loadsa love. E.

NOTE TO MS. TABITHA FROM POLLY PURRKINS, MATRON

It all ran very smoothly today, I'm pleased to say, but I need to speak to you URGENTLY. Mr. Catterie has raised concerns regarding Belle, one of the 1st Years. **P.**

QUICK NOTE : TABITHA FELINE TO PAWLENE McFURLEY, DEPUTY HEAD AND POLLY PURRKINS, MATRON :

Sherry tonight ? Trust it's nothing too serious about Belle. A busy day over - very successfully! Did Dora Catford tell you that Ms. Spitz collared Mr. Nepeta in the supermarket and gave him a long lecture on the Health and Safety aspects of erecting a maypole! The poor man was totally bemused as he had absolutely no idea why she thought he might be even remotely interested in maypoles! See you at dinner. T.

LETTER TO DR. TABITHA FELINE, C.B.E.

FROM THE CHAIRMAN OF THE ROYAL SOCIETY FOR THE PRACTICE OF CATS' ASSERTIVENESS, (R.S.P.C.A.), LONDON.

Dr. Tabitha Feline CBE,
St. Catte's Academy.

I have been requested by the Committee to invite you once again to address the forthcoming International Conference as our main Guest Speaker. Your work as an educationalist is well known of course, and it will be of great value to our delegates if you are able to fit the Conference into your busy schedule.

I look forward to meeting you again.

Yours sincerely,

Thomas Powercatt,

Chairman.

LETTER TO DR. THOMAS POWERCATT, CHAIRMAN, ROYAL SOCIETY FOR THE PRACTICE OF CATS' ASSERTIVENESS, (R.S.P.C.A.) , LONDON, FROM DR TABITHA FELINE.

Dear Dr. Powercatt,

R.S.P.C.A. International Conference

I have pleasure in accepting your invitation to address delegates at the Conference. In connection with our recent telephone conversation, as the emphasis this year is to be on the psychological aspects of Training for Life, I am able to confirm that my subject will be 'Human Behaviour Modification: Tactics and Techniques for Use by Kittens in the Training of their Humans.'

I look forward to hearing from you and receiving the full Conference programme in due course.

Yours sincerely,

Tabitha Feline

URGENT MESSAGE FROM MATRON TO ENID: Could you let Ms. Tabitha and Ms. McFurley have this ABSOLUTELY ASAP. Thanks.

URGENT MESSAGE FOR MS. TABITHA AND MS. PAWLENE McFURRLEY FROM MATRON

FOR YOUR IMMEDIATE ATTENTION :

URGENT - Mr. Catterie has confirmed the information regarding Belle. Matron will give you all the details when she sees you at lunch.

LETTER TO DR. LEO FELIX, PRINCIPUSS, ST. THOMAS COLLEGE

Dear Dr. Felix,

To confirm our telephone conversation of this afternoon, we were indeed somewhat surprised to learn that one of our latest arrivals, a delightful kitten called Belle who is hugely popular with the others in the class, should actually be called Bill. He is quite a character, bright as a button and with a pronounced sense of mischief. Mr. Catterie has given him a clean bill of health, and Matron, Ms. Purrkins, has had long chats with him and is confident that he understands the situation. I am sure he will settle in with you very quickly.

I was pleased and relieved that you have a vacancy and could take him, as I know that he will be in safe hands and will achieve his full potential at St. Thomas.

Thank you again for your help.

Yours sincerely,

Tabitha Feline

SIXTH FORM TEXTS :

Zo # wud u beleeeve BELLE IS NOW LITTLE BILL !!!!!

Rosie # wot?

Immi # wot?

Sam # wot?

Yaz # wot?

Zo # c u at break

NOTE TO ENID FROM TABITHA FELINE

Would you attach the Drama titles to the Agenda and send out. Thanks.

AGENDA - SENT TO ALL STAFF FROM TABITHA FELINE

<u>PLANNING MEETING : LITERARY FESTIVAL AND OPEN DAY</u>

<u>AGENDA</u>

Programme and running order

Activities and displays

Drama performances – list of suggested titles attached.

The judging of competitions: Art, Poetry etc.

Venues/locations/timetabling

Refreshments

MEMO : TO TABITHA FELINE FROM MS. MEWSING

As mentioned at the Planning Meeting, the Sixth Formers have completed their script and are well ahead with rehearsals for their production of 'A Midsummer Fright's Scream'. The work is excellent and it is 'amewsing' but I do have concerns about where some of the 'satire' is directed! A copy of their 'Hagbag' song is attached for your perusal.. They have very effectively adapted 'The Hag', one of the pieces which the choir sang at the recent Albert Hall Festival. Their next rehearsal is tomorrow afternoon if you are free.

M. Mewsing

SONG : THE HAGBAG

The hag is astride her broomstick to ride

With her batcat, and all dressed in leather.

She's thick and she's thin and if you let her in

You'll have storms and it won't be the weather.

A thorn in your fur, she'll stick like a burr

With words sharp as a bramble she rides now

Through fences and briars, this witch never tires

So it's best to take cover AND HIDE NOW.

MEMO : TO MS. MEWSING FROM TABITHA FELINE

I look forward to sitting in at the rehearsal tomorrow. It should be in interesting experience!!

Tabitha Feline

Email : to l.purrsey@vsc.net **and** moggym@topline.com **from** enid.p@setnet.com

Dear Mum, Dad, Auntie Daph and Mogs. We had the Open Day planning meeting today. Amazing how much organisation it will entail. Caitlin Kittsen's aerial athletics and extended leap team are going to do a display to show off the new gym area outside in the grounds, the choir are going to sing the pieces they sang in the Albert Hall recently in the massed choir festival, there's a poetry competition and three drama performances, and loads of other things. The Sixth Form tell me they have written their own version of Midsummer Night's Dream, called 'A Midsummer Fright's Scream', and they've included a song about a witch!! Wonder who that could be? They're worried now that they won't be allowed to do it.

Ms. Tabitha asked Mamselle if she would mind taking some of the other rehearsals and she immediately got very animated. Not absolutely sure what she said but it sounded like 'Zey learn to speak, zey learn to squeak. Zen zey need to pouffe. Zey need to bouffe. Zey need ze art dramatique.' Then she sort of 'flouffed' and 'rouffled' herself theatrically, presumably by way of a demonstration, and there was one of those long drawn-out 'Yes. Well. Right!' awkward silences, when we all looked down and didn't dare to look at each other in case someone caught someone's eye and laughed. It seemed to go on forever. Then Caitlin Kittsen asked something sensible and practical and we all breathed again, and the meeting proceeded. Can't wait to find out what Mamselle will be rehearsing! Whatever it is, it won't be dull, as she obviously sees herself as a bit of a 'Dancing Queen' lol!! Loadsa love. E.

NOTICE

**Rehearsals for an Open Day Demonstration of
MUSIC AND MOVEMENT
will be held in the gymnasium after classes
THIS AFTERNOON.**

Any kitten who is interested is invited to attend.

Signed : M'selle M. LaChatte

SIXTH FORM TEXTS :

Yaz # r u going to M'selle's dance rehearsal

Rosie # now THAT shd b an interestin experience!

Zo # why's she doing dancing

Sam # dunno, soon find out

Immi # OK c u there

NOTE : TO MS. TABITHA AND PAWLENE McFURLEY FROM MATRON

The kitten who limped into dinner after the dance rehearsal has sustained no serious damage. Over-enthusiasm and over-exuberance are the words which spring to mind, but then she IS one of the 3rd Years! I have asked M'selle to increase the warm-up time at the start of the sessions.

SIXTH FORM TEXTS :

Zo # are you goin to stick with M'selle's dance troupe

Rosie # nope

Immi # not likely

Sam # havin 3rd n 4th years crashin about tryin to be graceful is
DANGEROUS

Yaz # and hilarious!!!

QUICK NOTE TO PAWLENE MCFURLEY, DEPUTY HEAD, FROM MS. TABITHA

Have you any idea why the corridors and stairs suddenly seem to be far more crowded than usual with dawdling kittens being uncharacteristically quiet?

NOTE : TO MS. TABITHA FROM PAWLENE McFURLEY, DEPUTY HEAD.

Re: quiet corridors and dawdling kittens:

I think M'selle started off doing dance with the kits, as agreed, which developed into Music and Movement, and now seems to have 'transmog-giefied' into Performance Art. She is going to assemble a tableau of kittens, to represent 'the building blocks in the rhythm of life'. She did explain it all, rather volubly, but although I got the gist, I'm not sure I actually understand exactly what she means. However, she's very enthusiastic and the kits are keen. They're practising what M'selle calls 'stillness and pre-tab-leau micro-movement', thus the slow-motion. At least it's quiet. Apparently this involves curtain climbing practice, which of course, is part of Catlin's athletics programme. Up to now, Caitlin has been on hand to supervise but she has voiced concerns, so I've indicated that dance requires paws on the floor, and re-timetabled M'selle's sessions from the gym into the Main Hall where there are no curtains! As you're in London from first thing tomorrow morning, I thought I'd leave this for you now so you know the background in case it's discussed over dinner this evening. See you later. *P.*

Could you type up a draft of the attached rough notes for the R.S.P.C.A. Conference. No hurry, as I shan't be back until Friday. Pawlene McFurley will use my office as she will be keeping in touch with me on a daily basis while I'm away. Regards. TF

ROYAL SOCIETY FOR THE PRACTICE OF CAT'S ASSERTIVENESS (R.S.P.C.A.) CONFERENCE :

DRAFT NOTES

FULL TITLE : Psychological Aspects of Training for Life.

SESSION TITLE : Human Behaviour Modification - Tactics and Techniques for Use by Kittens in the Training of their Humans.

INTRODUCTION : Thanks, broad outline of Human Behaviour Modification, Tactics and Techniques for Use by Kittens in the Training of their Humans, rationale, context of training, background, overview etc.

LIVING AT HOME : It goes without saying that no cat would leave a good home without a reason, and no cat would stay in a home which is irretrievably unsatisfactory. However, if the Human cannot or will not be trained, then it may be necessary to look for somewhere else. Take your time about this, or opt for 'serial homing' - adopting 2 or 3 Humans who are needy, cat conscious, and with whom you are compatible, and then staying with each, in rotation.

FOOD : Food is extremely important in the training, control and management of the Human. They do not have an instinctive understanding of what is best for **you**, and are easily manipulated by manufacturers who make enormous profits from selling so-called catfood which is often 70% water and flavourings mixed into a sort of mousse. You will have to teach your Human to give you food which is acceptable to you and this is best done by trial and error. **You**, of course, know that cats prefer freshly cooked food, preferably straight from their Human's plate, or if necessary, from a newly opened tin/sachet/packet, but your **Human** will need careful training before accepting this fact. Never eat anything you do not like. Starve if you have to, which causes them great anxiety. If this does not produce the required quality of food, after a few days of refusal, eat what is put down for you then immediately throw it up again - on their feet or on the carpet. This will prove beyond doubt that the food does not agree with you and that they were entirely in the wrong to insist that you eat it against your better judgement, rather than starve. Your point will be made, your battle will be won, your Human will feel guilty, and you will be better fed.

Hygiene : Your dishes must be washed regularly. If your Human gets careless or doesn't pay sufficient attention to this, then obviously you will need to do something about it. Probably the easiest and most direct way is to leave a fairly thick layer of crumbly bits to dry like concrete in little brown lumps. They will soon learn to pick up and clean the dish right away, or invest in two dishes, one of which can be washed while you are using the other.

Leaving a clean dish : Clearing the dish entirely should only be done when:

1. The food is delicious.
2. You are starving and need every morsel to keep body and fur together.
3. You deem the attention being paid to your food is lacking and/or the food is too long delayed. The tactic here is to eat hungrily, then spend time carefully licking the saucer or dish. To press the point home, flip it over and lick the underside, then delicately hoover every tiny crumb from the floor, your paws, your chest. There won't be any, of course, but this is where a cat's capacity for acting comes in, which will be mentioned later. You will only do this, of course, when your Human is there to see it and be suitably chastened.

Eating at the table : Sharing a meal is sociable and companiable. Choose an occasion when your Human is eating alone. Sit on the table, at a discreet distance from the plate, and stare. Ease forward slightly and purr. When close enough, stretch out a paw and tap the plate. Purr louder. Inch closer and indicate what you fancy with a Silent Miaow, a paw-pat and a gently extended claw, still purring loudly. You will probably get the titbit, and a caress. If you are removed from the table, analyse your technique then wait for a suitable opportunity, and try again. Subtlety is the key to success.

Eating from the table : When your Human is eating at the table with the family or guests, a different technique is required - one just as subtle but much less obvious to others. Your Human has probably proclaimed that you are not to be fed from the table. Humans often make loud boasts about the discipline and training of animals, and probably believe what they are saying at the time, but this has little bearing upon their everyday actions. So sit under the table unobtrusively, close to your Human's feet and brush against them, or lean on them, or curl around them to draw attention to yourself. Your Human will take this as a sign of affection and you will probably get a caress or stroked. Purr loudly. Sit close to the legs and gaze up at him (this works best with the males), put your front paws on the chair then pat his leg, still purring. He will take this as a sign of adoration, will call attention to it and will ease you down to the floor. Continue leaning, patting and staring from under the table. If there is a tablecloth, peep out from under it and look appealing. Patience, purring and persistence will pay off. A sliver of something tasty will be unobtrusively slid down to you - and you will have established the precedent.

MANNERS : Humans have their own code of manners, which needn't concern us. Our good manners are instinctive and are demonstrated and taught to us by our mothers when we are tiny kittens. I would just mention one point. Humans consider it bad manners to play with their food. Cats consider it fun and good exercise.

SLEEPING : It is your right to sleep anywhere you please. Establish this early on. Your Human's bed is comfortable for stretching out on, or for drying yourself if you come in wet. Newly ironed clothes are a refreshing resting place. Remember your Human will boast about your idiosyncracies: sleep under the duvet, or find odd and interesting places - a drawer, a box, a bag, a vase etc., and cram yourself into them. They will be delighted. They will take photos and put them on YouTube and Facebook. Beware - cupboard and shed doors cannot always be opened from the inside and do not get wedged.

IDIOSYNCRACIES AND WINNING WAYS : Humans like to feel they are individuals and that their lives are 'special' and different, which is why they love to boast about their cat's cute characteristics. As kittens, we do this 'cuteness' sweetly and unconsciously. We are appealing and irresistible to all but the hardest anti-feline heart, but actually, we never lose this ability to tug the Human heartstring, to keep the emotional contact, to be fluffy and furry. Remember this - we make them happy, we give them something to talk about with their friends, we enhance their lives, we make them SPECIAL.

CHILDREN : Regard small children with great caution. They are inclined to be either frightened of you or over-exuberantly affectionate. Never scratch one. You don't know where it has been or what you might catch from it. Humans are incredibly protective of their young, as indeed are we. If a situation calls for claws, a gentle hint - a tiny tightening, should suffice. If that is not sufficient then leave immediately – up, down, under, through or over any obstacle. Speed is essential. Withdraw your favour by disappearing each time the child/children appear. This works well. They can't get at you, and your Human understands that the child has transgressed your boundaries of tolerance. Older children, well trained, can be affectionate and become good bedfellows and friends.

THE 'SILENT MIAOW', ACTING AND DRAMA : The Silent Miaow embodies pathos, poignancy, dependence and desolation. It is one of our most powerful tools, learned from our mothers when we are barely weaned. It is heartfelt so it is not just acting, but the way we make use of it consciously takes it into the realms of drama of the highest order. Use it, or lose it, kittens, but use it sparingly to give maximum effect. Our acting skills do not rest solely with the Silent Miaow. Our sensitivity, body language and sinuous movement make us able to convey mood and communicate clearly, and has a powerful effect upon the Human.

As an example, I will give just one possible scenario. Picture the scene. The house is quiet and dark. You open your eyes, dig claws into the lap you are sitting on (to ensure attention) and stare fixedly at something (anything: it doesn't matter what). You bristle your fur slightly, emit a small noise (any noise - a snore, sneeze, anything), and by this time you are centre stage and in the spotlight, so to speak, and have the complete attention of your Human. You could stand stiff-legged, howl, do the bottle-brush tail, anything you like. Be creative. Take it as far as you wish. It is surprising how many houses have been deemed haunted - with follow-up from the Psychic Society, TV coverage, book deals etc. - all because the cat was bored! It is necessary to consider the consequences though. When you feel the situation has gone far enough start the kitty-play and gambolling. This defuses their tension and completely destroys the ghost-hypothesis. If you are completely comfortable and at ease, so will your Human be. That is their reasoning.

CATS AND COMPUTERS : These do not really mix. Computers are uncomfortable to lie on, although sometimes this has to be done if your Human is spending too much time at the keyboard. The mouse is boring. If you knock it off, it just dangles. Good for a swing or two, but its play-value is limited to how long you want to keep on hitting it.

ENTERTAINING : Cats are not entertainers. As an adult, our function is to train our Human to provide a catisfactory home. As kittens, we are natural entertainers, endlessly fascinating to Humans. We cannot help attracting attention, and they 'coo' and burble at us as we, big-eyed little bundles of furry cuteness, absorb the lessons of life.

Cats do not do tricks. We do not offer a paw, jump over sticks or fetch balls unless we want to - and usually we don't. Cats do perform, beautifully - often when our Human has visitors, and for a very short time. We might, if we judge them to be bored and boring, sit in the centre of the room or on the window-sill, and do the ceremonial 'paw lick and over the ear' movement which they find fascinating. There is, of course, a world of difference between normal washing for hygiene and the elegant wash for effect, when we are aware of our admiring audience and can keep our Humans amused and charmed with our gracefulness. Or we might, if feeling frivolous, chase the tail round and round for a moment, playfully and prettily, which they find enchanting. Or we could bestow favour and sit upon someone's knee, although this has been known to produce Human hysterics.

If your Human has been particularly compliant and good, you might like to reward him/her with a little something extra in front of guests - climbing on the lap during a dinner party, say. Sit with your back to him/her, and gaze at the guests around the table in greeting. This will get a huge reaction - from smiling approval through absolute adoration to expressions of horror from the non-cat persons. Rub your head against him/her in an expression of affection as you are lifted off the lap on to the floor, sit where you are placed, purr loudly and I can guarantee a tasty titbit will be forthcoming.

AFFECTION : All cats know how to show affection. Humans have to be trained to receive and interpret our subtle signals. We do not need to fawn upon our Human, to leap up in an ecstasy of joy when they approach, as a dog does. A dog is TRAINED BY ITS HUMAN to do this, because it makes the Human feel good. A cat TRAINS ITS HUMAN to feel good merely by recognising whatever small gesture we offer :

1. A simple nose-to-nose greeting if they pick you up (with your permission, of course).
2. A small rub of the head against the ankle to acknowledge their presence
3. Merely accepting a tasty morsel of food with grace, and relishing it, makes your Human feel wonderfully powerful.
4. Just eating the food put down on your dish indicates that your Human has remembered your rules and is eager to please. A small 'broop' of thanks will be appreciated.

For some reason, holding the tail erect as you greet your Human will be interpreted as a sign of affection. It's a small enough gesture, and it keeps them happy.

As an extra token of your affection, from time to time you could offer your Human a small gift. A mouse say, or even a bird might be appreciated. They have an extraordinary and extremely noisy reaction to this sort of offering, and will, once again, boast about your thoughtfulness to their friends.

CONCLUSION : Humans feel they need to look after us. This makes them happy. Remember - a Happy Human is a Trained Human, trained by you. And how do we train our Humans. Do we manipulate them? Of course we do. Do we control them? How could we? Do we force? Coerce? Blackmail? No. Never. We guide our Humans. We know what is best for us, and what is best for us is ultimately best for our Humans, so that they can lead a catisfactory life. Vary your approach. There is no one way. You are the best judge. What your Humans see as your idiosyncracies, funny little ways and intriguing habits actually make THEM different, enhance their lives, and gives them something to talk about. They will boast to their friends and even to strangers that they have a Cat of Character. And we can enjoy the special and affectionate relationship with our Human which has flourished in our careful and caring paws.

SIXTH FORM TEXTS :

Yaz # HELP there's kits hangin all over the tapestry in the main hall

Sam # Wot

Immi # OMG

Zo # c u there

Rosie # get Catlin Kittsen QUICK

Email : from st.cattes@set.net.com to DR. TABITHA FELINE from Pawlene McFurley, Deputy Head

Slight contretemps late afternoon. M'selle's Performance Art tableau involved kittens hanging in serried ranks from the tapestry in the Main Hall, little 1st Years at the top down to 5th Years attaching themselves to the bottom. Spotted by 6th Formers, coped with by Catlin, banned by me on Health and

Safety grounds. Mr. Nepeta has checked the wall brackets which are OK , Matron has checked the kits, Dora Catford says the tapestry has sustained little damage, M'selle is not happy and NEITHER AM I. Apart from that - no news! Regards, P.

Email : to l.purrsey@vsc.net **from** enid.p@setnet.com

Hi. Sorry I missed your call. Had to stay late. There's a huge commotion going on. M'selle was supposed to be organising dance/music and move-ment, sort of Performing Arts I suppose, for Open Day, which she changed into Performance Art and had the kits attaching themselves in rows across the big tapestry in the Main Hall in a 'Kitten Curtain' tableau! Pawlene McFurley's furious and has vetoed the whole thing, M'selle got huffy and is not speaking to anyone and Ms. Tabitha's still away. Don't know any more - the Sixth Form will no doubt fill me in with all the details! Loadsa love. E.

NOTE : TO PAWLENE McFURLEY FROM POLLY PURRKINS, MATRON :

I keep finding kittens climbing far too high for safety and clinging to completely unsuitable surfaces. M'selle's obviously set off a new climbing craze. Glass of red tonight to discuss tactics? P.

IMPORTANT NOTICE

ALL CLIMBING ACTIVITIES MUST BE DISCONTINUED FORTHWITH OR THERE WILL BE SERIOUS CONSEQUENCES.

ONLY THE 'AERIAL ATHLETICS AND EXTENDED LEAP' TRAINING WITH MS. CATLIN KITTSEN, IN THE GYMNASIUM, IS PERMITTED.

Signed : *Pawlene McFurley,* **Deputy Head.**

Thanks to M'selle no doubt, a new climbing craze has emerged - kittens clinging precariously aloft everywhere. I have banned any sort of climbing activity outside the gym, M'selle has taken to her bed, and Catlin has doubled the AA and EL training sessions. Everything's in hand. Regards. P.

Dear Mum, Dad, Auntie Daph, Mogs and everyone. Tried to ring tonight but you were all out so decided to do the catch-up this way again. Well. Where to start. It's been a very odd couple of days. M'selle was totally out of order with her Performance Art pretensions, and had the kits CLIMBING UP THE TAPESTRY IN THE MAIN HALL! They were supposed to hang in rows like furry little pompoms with tails, small ones at the top down to bigger ones at the bottom, kits all colour co-ordinated in an intricate pattern according to fur shade! The Sixth Form, who have this uncanny way of knowing all the details of everything (and they're usually right), say that the idea was that all the little tail movements were to be synchronised, moving in rhythm like tiny metronomes, or a fluffy Mexican Wave!! But the tapestry swayed alarmingly as the bottom rows attached themselves and the kits at the top started to panic and squeak, not surprisingly, and were hanging on for dear life. The Sixth Formers saw what was happening and dashed off to get Catlin Kittsen who arrived to find M'selle about to throw a major wobbly. Ms. McFurley and Matron rushed onto the scene, plus Mr. Nepeta with his trusty ladder, but Catlin had by this time climbed up and she and the Sixth Formers were guiding the topmost ones down. The kits were fine but really giddy and thoroughly over-excited, Matron was calming them down and Mrs. Catford provided soothing milky drinks.

Then they discovered that Sofronia was missing. She's the one who's afraid of heights that Mr. Nepeta had to rescue from the tree. So of course there had to be a huge search and Catlin eventually saw Sofronia's little tail sticking out from the back of a radiator at the side of the stage. She was extracted with some difficulty as she'd really wedged herself in, and emerged with whiskers festooned in cobwebs and all covered in dust. Mrs. Catford was MOST put out at this evidence of lax housekeeping, but then Caitlin made her laugh by saying that Sofronia was more effective than the feather dusters which the kittens kept killing and why didn't Mrs. Catford use the 1st Years instead as they would probably enjoy all the scrambling about and would be so busy cleaning themselves afterwards that it might keep them out of trouble. Ms. McFurley has totally banned ANY sort of climbing ANYWHERE by ANYONE except under Catlin's supervision in the gym. She's not as tactful as Ms. Tabitha and M'selle got really huffy and hasn't been seen since, having taken to her bed and is too pawly/sick (i.e. outraged and sulking) to take her classes. Anyway, Ms. T is back tomorrow and will no doubt sort everything out. Off to bed. Speak soon. Loadsa love, E.

SIXTH FORM TEXTS :

Sam # Yay. Free lesson

Immi # Wot

Yaz # Mam'selle's sick

Zo # we're sick too.. of Mamselle!!

Rosie # make the most of it. Ms. T's back

QUICK NOTE TO PAWLENE MCFURLEY AND POLLY PURRKINS, MATRON, FROM TABITHA FELINE :

We need to revive M'selle, move her on from the 'kitten curtain' fiasco and give her something to concentrate on. I have some ideas but don't want to discuss them at dinner. Sherry afterwards? T.

QUICK NOTE : TO M'SELLE M. LACHATTE FROM TABITHA FELINE

Would you like to join me for coffee in the morning?

Regards,

Tabitha Feline.

SIXTH FORM TEXTS :

Yaz # Big meeting Mamselle and Ms. T

Immi # do u think she'll get fired

Sam # hope so

Zo # Nah

Rosie # soon see lol

QUICK NOTE : TO PAWLENE MCFURLEY AND POLLY PURRKINS FROM TABITHA FELINE

Just wanted to prime you before dinner. I asked M'selle to consider a different aspect of Music and Movement - a sort of Isadora Duncan/Greek Dancing, with absolutely NO CLIMBING. Pretty much as we discussed last night. She trained as a dancer apparently, so is knowledgeable about dance, and I'm not really QUITE sure where we're going with this, but we need to be positive about any suggestions she makes - hopefully she'll come up with some which we can all discuss at the table. Sherry later? T.

SIXTH FORM TEXTS :

Sam # OMG Mamselle's doing dance again

Zo # nooooooooo

Rosie # it's not exactly dance she's doing

Yaz # it's Greek dancin

Immi # Wot's that

Rosie # sort of floaty posey stuff

Sam # need to know more. Ears to the ground y'all

Email : to l.purrsey@vsc.net **from** enid.p@setnet.com

Dear Mum and Dad. Great to chat last night - pleased I caught you in! Forgot to tell you Mamselle's doing dance again!! She's made a miraculous recovery, emerged from her sick bed for a meeting with Ms T. and is starting Movement Art rehearsals. I've just pinned the notice up. No idea where this one will end up, but Open Day should be interesting!!! Are you going to come? Love E.

NOTICE

Rehearsals for an Open Day Performance of MOVEMENT ART will be held in the Minor Hall after classes THIS AFTERNOON.

Any kitten who is interested is invited to attend.

Signed : M'selle M. LaChatte

SIXTH FORM TEXTS

Rosie # just spoken to mamselle. It's Isadora Duncan-type dancing

Sam # wot's that

Immi # But Isadora Duncan got strangled when her scarf got caught in the car wheel

Yaz # excellent idea.. make ALL the 3rd n 4th years join

Zo # ha ha. Can't miss this. C y'all there.

QUICK NOTE TO POLLY PURRKINS AND PAWLENE MCFURLEY FROM TABITHA FELINE

Goodness! I see from M'selle's notice that we're doing Movement Art! What an extensive repertoire she has to offer! I look forward to a full account of today's rehearsal at dinner. T.

LETTER FROM DR. LEO FELIX, PRINCIPUSS, ST. THOMAS COLLEGE, TO DR. TABITHA FELINE

Dear Dr. Tabitha,

I thought you would be interested to hear about the progress young Bill is making. He is, as you said, a pleasant and sociable kitten and has done extremely well in the latest assessments. He is also fast becoming the star of our Aerial Athletics and Extended Leap team, which I feel is due, in no small measure, to his training with Ms. Catlin Kittsen. You must have been very pleased with the St. Catte's team performance at the recent District Competitions.

I hope you are well.

Yours sincerely,

Leo Felix

MEMO TO MS. CATLIN KITTSEN FROM TABITHA FELINE

I am enclosing a copy of a letter I received this morning from Dr. Felix, at the St. Thomas College. It is good to hear that little Belle-now-Bill has settled in and is making his presence felt in the A.A. and E.L. team so soon. It is also good that our team's achievements are recognised as the result of all the time and effort you have put in. Thank you.

Tabitha Feline

LETTER TO DR. LEO FELIX, PRINCIPUSS, ST. THOMAS COLLEGE, FROM TABITHA FELINE

Dear Dr. Felix,

Thank you for the update on young Bill. It is good to hear that he is settled and making progress, but not good to hear that our Aerial Athletics and Extended Leap team might have lost a star in the making!

I have passed your comments on to Catlin Kittsen.

Best regards,

Tabitha Feline

QUICK NOTE TO PAWLENE MCFURLEY DEP. HEAD AND POLLY PURRKINS, MATRON

I looked in on rehearsals this afternoon to see how it was all going. M'selle has certainly caught their attention - all sorts of 'Movement Art' going on. Mostly 5th Formers, but there were quite a few from the other years as well. The 6th Formers tell me 'It isn't quite their thing', which is predictable. I also popped in on Catlin's session, to congratulate the team again on their success at the District A.A and E.L events and on their qualifying for the Area competitions. They're going to be impressive in the Open Day displays. Catlin's got her sights on the Cat Commonweath Games eventually! T.

SIXTH FORM TEXTS :

Rosie # well that wz an interestin experience

Sam # not really one i'd want to repeat

Yaz # Ms. T comes in and mamselle goes all twittery and arty

Immi # She lost me when she went on about fluidity of motion

Sam # wot IS that

Yaz # Pawd knows but that's wot they'll be doing

Zo # according to mamselle, it's pouffing and bouffing n bein statuesque apparently

Rosie # Wot? The KITS?

Sam # oh it just gets better and better

Immi # so there we'll be, in mamselle's twirling little troupe. NOT

Yaz # ha ha, as if!!

Email : to moggym@topline.com **from** enid.p@setnet.com

Hi Mogs. Can't believe we were on the 'phone for so long, but a catch-up was DEFINITELY OVERDUE. Not sure about getting home this weekend as there's a lot going on for Open Day and I said I'd help, but to be honest, it's so hilarious I wouldn't miss it for worlds! I told you that after M'selle's 'kitten curtain' fiasco, Ms. T asked her to revert to the original music and movement idea, possibly to perform on Open Day, well she's now got the kits formed into a sort of Isadora Duncan/Greek dancing troupe. She's called it 'Movement Art', and it's all supposed to be measured movement and posing and swirling slowly about AND WE ARE TALKING ABOUT THE KITS HERE!! The 5th Years are really keen and go off on their own to practice because they say the younger ones get under their paws and don't take it seriously enough, which makes M'selle very voluble as she keeps losing half her troupe. Oh, there's never a dull moment. If you can't come before, you must try and be here for Open Day!! Speak soon, love E.

QUICK NOTE TO PAWLENE MCFURLEY AND POLLY PURRKINS FROM TABITHA FELINE

The corridors and stairs seem to be very slow-moving again, which has I presume, a connection with M'selle's dance. I think we might need tactics if we are to avoid another bout of artistic temperament! Sherry later? T.

MEMO : TO FORM TUTORS AND ALL STAFF FROM TABITHA FELINE

I am pleased to see so many kittens show so much interest in M'selle LaCh-atte's 'Movement Art', but would be glad if you would remind them that 'movement' means NOT STANDING STILL! Could I ask you all to walk around the corridors and stairs as often as possible between classes, and move the kits on when they get static. The Sixth Form are also going to assist. Thanks.

Tabitha Feline

NOTICE BOARD – MAIN HALL

PLEASE REMEMBER TO OBEY CORRIDOR AND STAIRCASE RULES – SINGLE FILE : NO RUNNING: AND NO DAWDLING.

Signed : Tabitha Feline

Email : to l.purrsey@vsc.net **from** enid.p@setnet.com

Hi Mum, Dad and Auntie Daph. Won't be home this weekend. Am helping out here with some of the Open Day stuff. Not sure what I'll be doing but can't wait to see! The play rehearsals all seem to be going well. Ms. Mewsing's very organised and I'm doing the prompting for a couple of them. Catlin's Aerial Athletics and Extended Leap team did hugely well in the District and are going into the Area competitions (I think I've got that right). She'd love to get them to Cat Commonwealth Games standard!! And these are the little blighters who not long ago kept hurling themselves over the garden wall in their mad version of Kitten Catapult!! M'selle's Movement Art is now sort of Isadora Duncan/Greek Dancing and the 5th Years absolutely love it. They have taken to M'selle's frouffing and posing with enthusiasm, and are draping themselves everywhere. Around every corner there are slow-moving kittens, drooping languidly over chairs and window sills, and stretching and stalking off, bouffing the tail and pouffing about and striking attitudes. Then of course, some of the 3rd and 4th Years joined in, and now we've even got the 1st and 2nd Years at it. They're supposed to descend a staircase elegantly, without looking down at their paws, which is all very well, but they tread on each other's tails then hiss and swipe each other, which rather spoils the effect. And of course, we daren't laugh because it all has to be taken seriously. It's a hoot. You are going to come for Open Day, though, aren't you? Loadsa love. E.

SIXTH FORM TEXTS :

Immi # 5th Yrs have formed a pop group called THE CATTERWAULS

Rosie # wot

Yaz # wot

Sam # wot

Zo # wot

Email : to enid.p@setnet.com **from** l.purrsey@vsc.net . **Subj. Open Day**

Dear Enid. Your Dad and I wouldn't miss it!! Open Day sounds as if it will be most intriguing. Auntie Daph says to tell you that Polly Purrkins has invited her so she's coming too, and says she's looking forward to recreating old times with her mate! Not sure I like the sound of that, if the tales she tells about their last week-end, or of their student days, are even half true! Take care, will 'phone later this week. Love Mum.

SIXTH FORM TEXTS :

Immi # Re 5th yrs. Nope. As u were. All's changed. They're now THE
CATTITUDES dance group

Rosie # wot

Zo # wot

Sam # wot

Yaz # wot

Immi # AND MAMSELLE SAID OK

Zo # OMG they'll be unbearable

Rosie # they're already clutterin the place up

Yaz # cattitudinising everywhere lol

Sam# RED ALERT.. Info needed. Will kitnap a 5th year and interrogate.
C y'all at lunch!

MEMO : FROM TABITHA FELINE

<u>TO ALL STAFF :</u>

There was so much languishing and drooping and draping going on outside the Dining Room this morning that we had a gridlock situation. Please display the following in every Form Room and draw the attention of EACH KITTEN to its contents. Thanks.

IMPORTANT NOTICE : Corridor and staircase rules are still not being observed. Single file, no running and no dawdling is allowed. Dancing or rehearsing dance-steps IN THESE AREAS IS STRICTLY PROHIB-ITED. Failure to comply with these rules will have serious consequences.

Tabitha Feline

NOTICE BOARD – MAIN HALL

BE WARNED

I SHALL HAVE NO OPTION BUT TO BAN ANY ACTIVITY WHICH CONTRAVENES HEALTH AND SAFETY REGULATIONS CONCERNING THE USE OF CORRIDORS AND STAIRCASES.

Signed : Tabitha Feline

QUICK NOTE : TO PAWLENE MCFURLEY DEP. HD. AND POLLY PURRKINS, MATRON

There are kittens draped upon every surface and round every corner, M'selle is looking very fraught and all this enthusiasm seems to be getting out of hand. Would you have a chat with all concerned to obtain a clear picture of what is going on, then can we discuss over sherry later? Thanks. T.

SIXTH FORM TEXTS :

Rosie # Free lesson first thing. Mamselle wasn't in

Yaz # wot

Zo # why

Rosie # dunno

Immi # she wz late for rehearsal as well

Zo # too much frouffing about

Sam # all that dance Not good for anybody

Yaz # I saw her coming in late last night

Sam # ooooo is there something goin' on? Ears to the ground y'all!

MEMO : TO ALL STAFF FROM TABITHA FELINE

Thank you all for the extra work you are undertaking in preparation for Open Day, which promises to be rather special this year. I see that many of the classroom displays are already in place. Catlin's Aerial Athletics and Extended Leap team are on top form, play rehearsals are going well and costumes etc. are all in hand. As you know, M'selle has decided upon a Greek theme for the dance troupe, who will stand motionless lining the main path and around the edges of the lawn until at a given signal, they will all move to the centre of the grass and perform. The Fifth Years will lead, and because so many of the younger kittens want to participate, Ms. Furlong has agreed to assist with rehearsals. Standing each kitten on a plinth like a statue, as M'selle suggested, would indeed look spectacular, but it is not possible for Mr. Nepeta to provide plinths. The Sixth Form have agreed to perform their play at the end of the afternoon, so they will be available to act as guides and do their official 'meeting and greeting' duties. They have offered to assist Mrs. Catford and her staff when required, as usual. Behaviour in the corridors and on the stairs is now much more orderly because of all the extra supervision you provided. Thank you again, and let me know if you have any concerns .

Tabitha Feline

SIXTH FORM TEXTS :

Yaz # MAYDAY MAYDAY SOS 3rd FORM DORM. NOW. UPROAR, they've seen a winged bat-like creature flying from branch to branch in the twilight

Rosie # ooer vampires am on my way

Immi # sounds like the 1st yrs again, better check their dorm

Zo # see u there

Sam # on my way to get matron

Email : to l.purrsey@vsc.net **and** moggym@topline.com **from** enid.p@setnet.com

You are not going to believe this! 3rd Years get themselves into a panic with mad tales of vampires, 1st Years suspiciously unaffected by this and quietly sleeping in their 'kitten cuddle' basket. Very suspicious Matron and Ms. McFurley do a search of their dormitory. Nothing found. All quiet. 6th Form still on duty. Giggling and squeaking heard. A second search. Ta Da!! Bill-who-used-to-be-Belle is discovered in the kitten cuddle basket covered by kits! He wanted to see his little friends, had sneaked out of St. Thomas's using his aerial-athletic-and-extended-leap skills, which are obviously considerable, and ended up here again. Unbelievable but true! There was lots of tutting, 'phone calls were made and young Bill was returned to St. Thomas. Who would have thought it! Little Belle! Well, she always was a handful! The whole school was buzzing the next morning except M'selle, who had apparently slept right through it. For someone who had a good night's sleep when the rest of them were agog and unsettled, she looked remarkably tired this morning. Perhaps she really IS pawly. Loadsa love. E

SIXTH FORM TEXTS :

Zo # OMG the Cattitudes are going to be GREEK STATUES

Rosie # wot

Immi # wot

Sam # wot

Yaz # wot

Zo # they're in the garden now C u there

Email : to l.purrsey@vsc.net **and** moggym@topline.com **from** enid.p@setnet.com

It's all happenin' here! This place is buzzing! There's rehearsals, practices and preparation going on everywhere. M'selle's Movement Art has sort of moved into Greek dancing and she asked Mr. Nepeta to make plinths, and me to order sort of floaty material to make veils. There is a sort of logic there. Plinths. Greek statues. Greek dances. Greek dancing on the lawn. But kittens with veils? The Sixth Form swear she's teaching them the Dance of the Seven Veils and the mind promptly boggles! Anyway, dances with veils they are doing. ALL the kits in the dance troupe. The little ones keep pouncing on each other's veils and end up in furry tangled heaps, then have to be carefully extricated without strangling themselves or each other. I've had to order more veil-stuff already. They keep shredding them. It's hilarious and all hands on deck at times to sort them out, but M'selle's not quite her volatile self, although she is still shrugging and 'froufing' a lot. The 'Cattitudes' are striking poses everywhere. M'selle has seized the opportunity of including a tableau (she's determined not to let that idea go!), and Miss Furlong's been roped in to help Ms. Mewsing with the task of organising them into standing in Greek poses and they are to border the path and lawn like Greek statues (but without the plinths, incidentally), which is pretty far-fetched as the only time the little ones are still is when they're asleep. Oh dear, it is funny but I mustn't laugh. I can't wait for you to come and see this on Open Day! Loadsa love. E

LETTER TO DR. TABITHA FELINE FROM DR. LEO FELIX, PRINCIPUSS, ST. THOMAS COLLEGE

Dear Dr. Tabitha,

I should like to express my thanks once again to you and your staff for all your efforts in retrieving young Bill and returning him to us. The whole situation could obviously have had very serious consequences. We still have no clear idea as to how he managed his escape, as he was definitely in his basket in his dormitory at 'lights out'. He has demonstrated the route he took, which looks quite impossible but is obviously within his capabilities. Could we avail ourselves of Ms. Catlin Kittsen's expertise in this field, and ask for her assistance in ensuring that there is no repeat performance of this escapade, by Bill or anyone else. Thank you again.

I trust you are well.

Yours sincerely,

Leo Felix

Principuss.

Email : to enid.p@setnet.com **from** l.purrsey@vsc.net

Dear Enid. Dad and I are really looking forward to coming down. Your Auntie Daph is making detailed and very involved plans for nights out with Polly Purrkins over this Open Day week-end. I've just told her not to expect your Dad and I to accompany them and she's cackling away saying what makes me think they'd want us! I ask you - is this the sort of thing you expect from mature females of uncertain age, even if they haven't had a night out together for ages? Auntie Daph says she's not past her sell-by date yet, and you can go with them if you like as you'll know all the best clubs. For goodness sake! You'd think they were teenagers!! Dear oh dear, I just know this is going to end badly!!!! Hope all's going well. Take care. Love Mum.

Email: to l.purrsey@vsc.net **from** enid.p@setnet.com

Ha ha!! I think I'll 'pass' on the clubbing-with-Auntie-Daph idea. Lol. Mad rush! Loadsa love. E

LETTER TO DR. LEO FELIX, PRINCIPUSS, ST. THOMAS COLLEGE, FROM DR. TABITHA FELINE

Dear Dr. Felix,

Thank you for your letter. We were all very relieved that Bill's escapade had no serious consequences. Our First Years are enormously proud of his achievement and have dubbed him 'Batboy Bill'. One can only trust that he has no ambitions to utilise his talents by becoming a cat-burglar!

Ms. Kittsen says that she will be pleased to offer any assistance she can. Perhaps you would contact her direct to make mutually convenient arrangements.

Best regards,

Tabitha Feline

SIXTH FORM TEXTS :

Rosie # M'selle's not in class

Yaz # wot again?

Zo # that's twice this week

Immi # wot's going on

Sam # who cares. Free lesson. Yay

Email : to l.purrsey@vsc.net **and** moggym@topline.com **from** enid.p@setnet.com

Dear all. Well, Mr. Nepeta was very relieved to hear he hasn't got to make plinths for M'selle's Greek statues, and WE were all very relieved to hear that we weren't going to have to run around catching kittens who were toppling off them. Win/win all round! I had coffee with him and Mrs. Catford. Apparently he brings her a little something from the garden each day, flowers or veg - at the moment it's strawberries. Do you know - I think he's quite keen on Mrs. C! They have most of their meals together and it all looks very cosy when they're sitting there. 'Ooooo', as the 6th Formers would say, 'Something going on..!' They're such gossips! Rehearsals are going well, except you can't move in the garden without encountering kittens with 'Cattitude' standing posing, or trying to drift gracefully across lawns. There seems to be more of the Mamselle frouffy flounce there than a graceful drift at the moment, but they're all really keen. The veils are getting very tattered but Ms. T. says not to issue any more until the final Open Day rehearsal as they're on their second lot already. The 1st Yrs. are now trailing about with long shredded remains, and try to pinch the 5th Yrs' veils which are still more or less intact. Play rehearsals are shaping up well, except for King Ear's crown which won't stay on. In 'A Tail of Two Kitties', the citizens' woolly caps were too big and kept falling down over their eyes, so they couldn't see where they were going and were milling about and falling over each other. Ms. Mewsing and I spent ages yesterday making them smaller - the caps not the kittens, of course. The kits are pretty small already lol!! Oh, and there was the incident in 'The Tempuss' when Ariel (one of Catlin's AA and EL team), demonstrating her 'I go, I go' move rather over-enthusiastically, hurtled offstage straight into the rhododendrons, and had to be retrieved, squealing loudly, by Mr. Nepeta, who wasn't too pleased as he wants everything looking its best for Open Day, and there is now definitely a kitten-shaped hole in his floral display! Ms. Mewsing is everywhere - rehearsing the choir, the plays and the dance practices that M'selle doesn't take. We hardly see M'selle apart from when she's rehearsing her group. She's still frouffing about but seems sort of distracted, somehow. Sort of lost some of her fizz. She's still spending a lot of time on her own, working out more dance routines in the gym, the 6th Form tell me. No wonder she's looking tired. Talking of which, better go before I fall asleep. Loadsa love, E.

QUICK NOTE : to Pawlene McFurley, Deputy Head, and Polly Purrkins, Matron : from Tabitha Feline.

Interesting telephone call this afternoon! Enid is distributing the attached to the Staff so we can get their views over dinner. The question is - do we want a new pupil at this stage and can the staff cope with the extra work? Discuss in detail later, over sherry? T.

MEMO : TO FORM TUTORS AND ALL STAFF FROM TABITHA FELINE

I have had a telephone call from Laurent Goyarde's P.A. Yes, THAT Laurent Goyarde, the fashion designer. He has written a book in which his cat Chouette describes her life of high-flying fashion. He is embarking on a world publicity tour, travelling by private jet, and Chouette, his cat-companion, will accompany him. He has asked if we would take Sapphira, the kitten, while he is away.

Accepting a temporary pupil is not something I would normally contemplate, but it is possible Sapphira may join us on a permanent basis. I should like your comments before I make a decision, particularly in view of all the extra work you are undertaking in preparation for Open Day. I rather got the impression that M. Goyarde's reluctance to take Sapphira has more to do with her lively disposition than any concern about travel-sickness or her losing education time!

Perhaps we could discuss it over dinner. Thanks.

Tabitha Feline

SIXTH FORM TEXTS :

Rosie # to Immi #, Sam #, Yaz #, Zo # : BIG NEWS. Heard Matron tellin Mrs. C we've got a new 1ˢᵗ Year starting soon. Very posh apparently.

NOTICE BOARD – MAIN HALL

WILL THE KITTENS WHO FESTOONED THE MAIN STAIRCASE WITH THEIR DANCE VEILS PLEASE REMOVE THEM.

VEILS ARE NOT TO BE WORN EXCEPT FOR DANCE CLASSES. PLEASE HAND THEM IN TO M'SELLE OR MS. MEWSING AFTER REHEARSALS.

PLEASE REMEMBER CORRIDOR AND STAIRCASE RULES – SINGLE FILE, NO RUNNING, NO DAWDLING, NO DANCING.

Signed : Tabitha Feline

NOTE : TO POLLY PURRKINS, MATRON, FROM PAWLENE McFURLEY, DEPUTY HEAD

I am slightly concerned about M'selle. She hasn't been joining us in the Common Room in the evenings, goes to her room after dinner and no-one sees her until she appears in the morning. She has missed some classes, been late for others and is forgetting details like collecting the veils after classes, etc. It's bad enough having the corridors cluttered with the 'Cattitudes' without being ensnared in tattered fluttering veils at every corner. Could you have a chat? Find out what's going on? Thanks. **P.**

SIXTH FORM TEXTS :

Zo # just seen mamselle in the gym, dancing on her own WITH HUGE COLOURED FEATHERS

Rosie # OMG not feather frouffings with 1st years

Sam # 1st years and FEATHERS. Is she MAD?

Yaz # yes definitely

Immi # gotta see this.

Yaz # C y'all in the gym

NOTE: TO PAWLENE McFURLEY FROM POLLY PURRKINS

Had a word with M'selle. She says she is fine. Busy, of course, and has been working on some new dance ideas. Has missed breakfast a few times because she's been out early. I said we were concerned because she looks tired and doesn't seem quite her usual self. She assured me that she is feeling fine, says there is no cause for worry and all will be well after Open Day. **P.**

QUICK NOTE : to Pawlene McFurley from Tabitha Feline

Pawlene: Enid tells me there is a rumour circulating among the kittens that M'selle is introducing feathers into the Open Day dance routines. We are barely coping with the veils! Feathers are definitely forbidden. I don't want to intervene personally or make an issue of this, particularly as she seems to be showing signs of strain. Would you ask around and find out? Thanks. T.

Email : to moggym@topline.com **from** enid.p@setnet.com

Mogs. Oh, no! Got your message. Are you feeling O.K.? Will ring you this evening. Devastated you can't come. Hope you feel better soon. Take care. Love E.

Email : to l.purrsey@vsc.net **from** enid.p@setnet.com

Dear Mum and Dad. Thanks for your message. Poor Mogs!! It's such a pity she'll miss the Open Day weekend. I'm really disappointed. I thought that we'd both had chicken pox - at the same time if I remember rightly. Can you get it twice? Oh, yes, and BIG NEWS! We've got a new kitten starting and guess who enrolled her - only LAURENT GOYARDE, the fashion designer. Coo! What about that! Loadsa love. E

SIXTH FORM TEXTS:

Rosie # to Immi #, Zo #, Sam #, Yaz # New kitlet arrives this morning. Guess who her Human is. ONLY LAURENT GOYARDE FASHION DESIGNER !!!!! Volunteered us to look after her

NOTE : TO TABITHA FELINE FROM PAWLENE McFURLEY, DEPUTY HEAD

With regard to your query. Ms. Mewsing assures me that the dance programme is unaltered, there are no plans to change it and that rehearsals are going well. I had a word with M'selle who was rather vague about the feathers. She is indeed working on new dance routines but says that this is a personal project and won't involve the kits. However, I do have a slight worry – is she going to hurtle in wearing feathers and whirl about doing an impromptu extravananza during Open Day, like the astonishing twirling ribbon fandango performance after the kits had their health checks? We can only hope not - and keep a close watch...! **P.**

SIXTH FORM TEXTS :

Rosie # got called out of class by Ms. Mac to meet the new kit. Very very POSH. Louis Vuitton luggage.

Sam # who's Louis vuitton?

Rosie # brought her own dishes

Zo # bet Matron was pleased!

Rosie # and a set of menus

Yaz # Ole Catfood would love that

Immi # wot's her name

Rosie # Sapphira. you'll meet her at break

Sam # the kits will just call her Posh

Email : to l.purrsey@vsc.net **and** moggym@topline.com **from** enid.p@ setnet.com

Hiya Mum, Dad, Auntie Daph and poor old Mogs. I told you about the new kitten - well, she was delivered by fashion designer Laurent Goyarde HIMSELF. It was all very low key, of course, except that she arrived with loads of Louis Vuitton luggage, her own personal dishes, a complete set of menus for the chef (i.e. Mrs. Catford), and her own bedding! Most of this is now stowed away in Matron's 'Personal Effects' store. The 6th Formers say she isn't too posh at all, which is just as well, as the 1st Yrs would soon sort that out. Difficult to have airs and graces if you are at the bottom of the pile in the kitten cuddle basket and they all sleep on top of you!! There are rehearsals going on all over the place and Mr. Nepeta has organised a platform at one end of the lawn where the V.I.P's can sit. It has an awning which can be pulled down in case it's wet or too sunny. If it's windy, pawd 'elp us! It might take off ha ha. M'selle's apparently taken to rehearsing with feathers according to the 6th Formers, but they're such gossips! They've prob- ably just seen her trying out new steps now she's doing dance with the kits. Eek – the kits dancing with feathers! That would be fun..! Hope to be home this weekend. Loadsa love. E.

QUICK NOTE TO PAWLENE MCFURLEY AND POLLY PURRKINS from Tabitha Feline

How has the new arrival settled in? T.

NOTE: TO MS. TABITHA FROM MATRON

Er - Sapphira is not too bad, considering! She's not looking quite as pristine as when she first came, but IS slowly getting used to the idea that she has to groom herself and eat and sleep with the others. She's obviously used to more palatial surroundings. There was a slight difficulty when she occupied the cuddle basket thinking it was meant just for her and she was extremely put out when ALL the kits piled into it with her, so some predictable hissing and swiping went on. She then opted for her own bed and bedding, but I noticed last night that she had joined the others. She's eating well- and not from the menus provided by her chef. Dora has borrowed them, but I don't think she was impressed. Regards, **Polly.**

NOTE : TO MS. TABITHA FROM PAWLENE McFURLEY, DEPUTY HEAD.

As anticipated, Sapphira has been renamed 'Posh' by the kits and seems quite happy with that. She has apparently had a Personal Tutor up to now. Her work is up to standard. She mixes well with the other kittens although she seems to have very little idea about obeying rules, but of course, it is early days and the 6th Form are keeping a close but friendly eye on her which should keep her out of trouble. She and Sofronia seem to get on quite well, and Catlin and Ms. Mewsing are trying to give her a role in the Open Day preparations. We've had a couple of flashes of imperiousness , but Ms. Mewsing's pleased with her performances with the choir – she has quite a promisingly piercing miaow apparently, 'frouffes' most convincingly like M'selle (to the extent that I think there would appear to be quite an element of mimicry there!), and Catlin says she is showing promise in Aerial Athletics and Extended Leap, despite a very reluctant start. **Pawlene.**

LETTER : TO DR. TABITHA FELINE CBE, FROM MS. TRISTIA SPITZ

TRISTIA W. SPITZ

Dear Dr. Tabitha,

From all accounts, preparations for the Literary Festival and Open Day are going very well.

I have heard interesting news from a reliable source that you have a new pupil - with very close connections to a famous personage from the fashion world who will actually be attending the Academy Open Day. What an honour for St.Catte's! I look forward to meeting this distinguished visitor and hope that the fine weather holds for the big day!

I trust you are well,

Yours sincerely.

Tristia W. Spitz

QUICK NOTE TO POLLY AND PAWLENE: Thanks for the update on Sapphira. A missive has arrived from Ms. Spitz. Sherry later? T.

LETTER: TO MS. TRISTIA SPITZ FROM DR. TABITHA FELINE CBE

Dear Ms. Spitz,

Thank you for your letter. Preparations for the Literary Festival and Open Day are well under way, and like you, we hope that this warm dry spell continues. We are hoping to have our usual throng of interested and involved visitors, but are not expecting any celebrities of any sort to attend. In fact, I would probably discourage that, as it would take the focus from the hard work put in by staff and pupils!

I hope you are well, and will no doubt see you on Open Day.

Yours sincerely,

Tabitha Feline

Email : to l.purrsey@vsc.net **and** moggym@topline.com **from** enid.p@ setnet.com

Hiya. WitchSpitz's revving up for Open Day. She obviously heard something about Sapphira the designer kitten, got hold of entirely the wrong end of the stick, and assumed that we'd have a famous fashion designer attending Open Day, no doubt with the media and mad press people as well! I bet she was hoping for an introduction, lol. Sapphira's been renamed 'Posh' by the kitlets, which is what everyone now calls her and she doesn't seem to mind. It's all a bit manic, Ms. T's still sending loads of 'quick notes' out, there's rehearsals all over the place, Mr. Nepeta says if it rains all his flowers will be ruined and if it doesn't they'll be ruined anyway, Dora Catford is baking like mad in flurries of flour for the refreshments, Catlin's Aerial Athletics lot are doing their extended leaping everywhere possible (and impossible), the Cattitudes are still draping themselves languidly and bouffing their tails and pouffing about striking poses and falling over the 1st Yrs, M'selle is hardly seen and I doubt if I'll make it home this weekend. Never mind, not long now and Mogs, I'll tell you all about it. Every fascinatin' detail! That probably sounds more like a threat than a promise ha ha. Love. E.

SIXTH FORM TEXTS :

Sam # just taken some post up to Enid. Why r they addressed to
Dr. T CBE

Zo # cos she's got a CBE

Sam # yes but wot IS a CBE

Rosie # an honour

Immi # from the queen

Yaz # means CAT OF THE BRITISH EMPIRE

Sam # but we haven't got an empire

QUICK NOTE TO PAWLENE McFURLEY FROM TABITHA FELINE

Pawlene, I shall be VERY interested to have your comments on the attached!!!

LETTER FROM : THE LEARNING CONNECTIONS GROUP TO DR. TABITHA FELINE CBE

Dear Dr. Feline,

We should like to invite St. Catte's Academy to host one of our summer courses.

We harness course members' own abilities to reflect upon their strengths in order to focus upon their achievable goals.

The course is led by our inspirational specialist, Agnetha Fey, who is renowned in the development of Mindfulness and the Inner Self. The course description is enclosed.

For more information, enquiries and bookings, please contact Mystere Greene on 0279 2044 7044.

Yours sincerely,

Jonothan Astleer

LEARNING CONNECTIONS

ACHIEVE REALITY IN LEARNING

by harnessing the power of sustained mental focus

Experiential connection with individual learning resonances through

1. Meditation
2. Inspiration
3. Exploration
4. Imagination
5. Expression
6. Sensation

Using methods old, methods new, little known, tried and true

physical and practical.

PAUSE TO PONDER

STAY TO WONDER

MOVE ON – ENERGISED IN BODY, SPIRIT AND MIND.

MEMO TO MS. TABITHA FELINE FROM PAWLENE McFURLEY

This is utter rubbish! What exactly is it supposed to MEAN? WE pay THEM for the sessions? I think you should invite them to come and run an initial session, free of charge, so that they can demonstrate their methodology to us. It would be interesting to see them trying to apply this pretentious twaddle to our lively kittens in a genuine learning environment. It would be even more interesting to see them, having discovered the kits' talent for creating chaos, trying to cope with their own 'experiential connection with individual learning resonances' afterwards, and then see if they can 'move on energised in body, spirit and mind'! 'BATTERED in body, spirit and mind' might better describe it! Would they ever be the same again, I wonder. Complete claptrap.....! I'll hand the info. back to Enid. P.

SIXTH FORM TEXTS :

Rosie # Mamselle's not here again

Immi # she's not here either

Zo # she's not in the gym

Yaz # she wasn't in for breakfast again

Rosie # what is going on

Sam # I think she's pregnant

Rosie # wot?

Zo # wot?

Immi # wot?

Yaz # wot?

Email : to l.purrsey@vsc.net **and** moggym@topline.com **from** enid.p@ setnet.com

I'm really looking foward to seeing you down here this weekend - and Mogs wish you could come too. I won't be working late on Friday evening, but will be on duty on Saturday. You don't have to spend all Saturday afternoon at the school. You can pop in to have a look around for a while and then go. I'm a bit worried that you might find it all very boring. Just had an email from Auntie Daph asking for the best places for a night out on Saturday! I said we were going to enjoy a quiet meal together and she says she knows about that but what about afterwards! What is she like! I just can't imagine her and Matron in disco gear doing the rounds of the clubs. Well, I CAN imagine it – I just don't want to… lol. Everything's fine here. Mad busy - there's so much going on. Ms. T 's invited me to have dinner with them in the dining room this week as we've been working so late. Being included as one of the team is great and Mrs. C's food is fantastic. Don't know why the kits call her 'Catfood'. Because they're kits and they can, I suppose. The food is amazing. She always joins the other staff for coffee after dinner and sometimes Mr. Nepeta does too. I'm really enjoying all this. Oh, and the latest 6th Form gossip is that M'selle must be pregnant because she's missed breakfast a few times, is always late and keep forgetting things. They're such nosey little busybodies! I'm looking forward to seeing you here at the week-end. Mogs - it's such a shame you can't come. Hope you're beginning to feel better - and promise you will come as soon as you can. I'm sure you are absolutely inconsolable that you're missing all the excitement of Open Day....NOT.... lol. Loadsa love. E.

Email : to enid.p@setnet.com **from** l.purrsey@vsc.net

Stop worrying. We're all looking forward to it. Mogs sends her love. See you on Friday. Love, Mum. XX

SIXTH FORM TEXTS :

Rosie # am at 1st Yrs rehearsal in the gym. No mamselle. No veils. No keys. Is Ms. Mewsing there?

Immi # No, will find her

Sam # Music room, choir practice, just follow the noise

Yaz # I'll get Catlin

Zo # Catlin's here. On our way.

Rosie # it's ok. Mamselle's turned up

QUICK NOTE : TO PAWLENE MCFURLEY FROM TABITHA FELINE

Why do I keep seeing Sofronia leaping on top of things? She's like a furry little grasshopper! I know Catlin has been working with her to overcome her fear of heights, which I imagine has some connection with the fact that I have just found her clinging precariously but determinedly to the virginia creeper by the main door. Astonishing! She was somewhat evasive and said that yes, it was a bit scary but that she was 'increasing her aerial awareness before Open Day'. All part of a well laid plan? Regards, T.

MEMO : TO MS. TABITHA FELINE FROM PAWLENE McFURLEY, DEPUTY HEAD.

Had a word with Catlin. Sofronia has a special and secret 'task' and is working very hard to prepare for it. She is going to climb up to the balustrade above the main door to release the 'Welcome' banner on Open Day. Catlin IS keeping a careful watch on her and either she or Mr. Nepeta is actually close by when she 'trains', the idea being that she has the confidence to climb on her own. The Sixth Form are also assisting in keeping a discreet eye on Sofronia, which supervision they are choosing to call 'Covert Operation Aerial', so if you see them hiding under bushes or creeping about in a suspicious cloak-and-dagger way, that will be why. Sapphira has included herself in the extra training but is not allowed to climb on her own yet. Regards, P.

Email : to moggym@topline.com **from enid.p@setnet.com**

Mum and Dad are on their way and will be here in a couple of hours. Wish you were able to come with them! How're you feeling? Bit better, I hope. Just had a text from Auntie Daph about tomorrow. OMG. Matron and Auntie Daph on a girls' night out! Clubbing!! Wearing disco gear!!! Nooooooo! Something anyone in their right mind would definitely want to miss. She's still hoping to meet Matron tonight but Matron'll probably be on duty I would think. The kits are a bit hyper. Catlin organised a fun-run earlier, and they're now in the middle of a stair ping-pong competition. I can hear them all out there now. Each team bashes a ping pong ball up or down the stairs and scores points when they beat the ball as they run up or down the staircase. They all enjoy it hugely and it gets very very noisy. The kits get very excited and rush around a lot, which is the whole idea, really. Then they'll be ready for bed. Will keep you posted as to what's going on. I know you will be riveted by all the excitement, and will be waiting with baited breath for every interesting little detail....NOT....!! Lol. Loadsa love. E.

SIXTH FORM TEXTS :

Zo # Sofronia's stuck in the Virginia creeper again

Yaz # ok am In the gym. I'll get her

Sam # on my way but why's she doing all this climbing suddenly

Rosie # Doh!! Open Day task for Catlin of course

Zo # OMG Posh is up there with her

Immi # ok, on our way

Email : to moggym@topline.com from enid.p@setnet.com

Hiya Mogs. Would you believe - it's Saturday morning, it's Open Day and suddenly I've got nothing to do. The calm before the storm!! The visitors will be arriving in about half an hour, Mum and Dad and Auntie Daph included. I'm feeling nervous! It's daft to be this immersed in work, but you can't help getting involved and it's all very different from my last job and much more interesting. We had a quick run through the programme this morning and it went quite well. King Ear's crown is now tied on so it stays put, and there were a few forgotten lines, of course, and that's why they've got me prompting, but no-one crashed off the stage or banged into the scenery or anything. Sofronia did her practice climb up to the balustrade to release the 'Welcome' banner - and didn't get stuck or fall off. So why am I nervous? Because kittens cause chaos, that's why...lol..!. Pawlene McFurley says she is going to keep a close eye on M'selle to make sure it's only the kits that dance but I guess she'll be too busy keeping kittens' toes away from kittens' tails to start improvising! E.

Email : to moggym@topline.com from enid.p@setnet.com

Aunty Daph and Matron went out 'on the town' hours ago, all dolled up and they're still not back! Mum and Dad have gone to bed and it's time I did too. Hate to think what they're up to. I feel as if I'm their mother...!!! E.

Email : to moggym@topline.com **from** enid.p@setnet.com

IT IS NOW 2.30 A.M. AND AUNTIE DAPH AND MATRON HAVE ONLY JUST TOTTERED IN, giggling helplessly, insisting that they'd seen M'selle in the cabaret at the Club Exotique! As far as we could make out, she was the STAR OF THE FLOORSHOW and was called Fifi. Feathers and a partner called Fernando featured heavily in this tale and when they said hello after the performance, she got very excited and very voluble and burst into an encore. We couldn't actually follow the rest of their story as it all got a bit too confused and complicated for us to decipher, but they obviously had a great night out! They've all gone to bed now at last – and guess who's ended up sleeping on the settee!! Auntie Daph is a complete nightmare and Polly Purrkins is just as bad!!!! 'Night. E

SIXTH FORM TEXTS :

Immi # why is mamselle getting into a taxi with loads of suitcases?

Rosie # wot?

Sam # wot?

Yaz # wot?

Zo # wot?

QUICK NOTE : TO PAWLENE MCFURLEY AND POLLY PURRKINS FROM TABITHA FELINE

I have received a note from M'selle who appears to have left the premises some-time in the early hours of this morning. Could we discuss this urgently before it becomes common knowledge. Dora is bringing coffee to my office now. Thanks. T.

Email : to moggym@topline.com **from** enid.p@setnet.com

Well! Last night was interestin'!! A really unexpected end to all the excite-ment (?) of yesterday afternoon. which all went very well, starting with Sofronia's solo climb up the virginia creeper to unroll the banner which had been made by the 5th Formers, saying 'Welcome to St. Catte's Open Day'. She was just a bit wobbly and the 6th Form sort of formed a guard-of-hon-our-cum-safety-blanket underneath in case she slipped. I saw Sam holding

Posh very firmly in front of her, in case she shinned up as well to share the applause. Catlin's Aerial team were amazing and I heard one of the Governors saying the new Athletics Area was 'a sound investment'. Triumph!! Ms. T. will be pleased. All the plays went well, slight hitches here and there but no major catastrophes (pun intended lol). The 6th Form's spoof 'Midsummer Fright's Scream' was very funny, greatly appreciated by all the kits, who really enjoyed the 'Hag' speeches, and of course WitchSpitz was applauding and actually smiling, obviously with no idea that it was her, which made it even funnier! It was very cleverly done. M'selle's Greek Dancing groups were really impressive. The 5th Form 'Cattitudes' were having a wonderful time during their performance, drifting gracefully (yes, really!) and pouffing and frouffing their veils and tails about and posing and striking attitudes to great effect. The younger kittens were really good, too, on the whole. Not many pile-ups although a couple of the little ones got a bit enmeshed in the veils and had to be discreetly removed and disentangled by Matron and Ms. Mewsing. But the whole Cattitudes' display was amazingly graceful. They sort of oozed onto the lawn and swayed and drifted about with the veils billowing in the breeze. The choir were singing as a background to all this, which was sort of - I don't know, suitably atmospheric. I noticed Pawlene McFurley keeping very close to M'selle in case she donned feathers and hurtled about doing a 'dans exotique' but she showed no signs of joining in. Obviously saving her energy for later, as we now know!!

There was a slight incident at the end of all the performances, after Ms. T. had thanked everyone for coming and announced that refreshments were being served. Sofronia, obviously flushed with the success of her banner climb, had been dared by Posh to climb up on the awning over the platform, and at that moment WitchSpitz strode purposefully across the platform, seized the microphone and started to propose an impromptu and entirely unexpected vote of thanks, uncalled for and completely unnecessary as the Chairman of the Governors had already done it and all the speeches were over. As Sofronia stood on the awning above WitchSpitz, Posh appeared and Sofronia pounced on her, slipped, slid slightly forward and her weight tilted the awning which came down very, very slowly like a curtain. Inch by inch WitchSpitz disappeared from view. Mr. Nepeta, who seems to have a sixth sense in foreseeing impending kitten-created problems, promptly set about raising it, and WitchSpitz, still graciously talking, gradually reappeared, but her audience, with Mrs. Catford's cakes in mind, were turning away and moving off for their tea. The 6th Formers coped admirably, retrieving

Sapphira and Sofronia, removing them swiftly and unobtrusively from the scene, and then forming an escort to usher WitchSpitz firmly towards the dining room. Astonishing - Sofronia, who hates heights in trouble for climbing!! But that's kittens for you! You never know what they'll do next! She and Posh had to assist Mr. N with the clearing up as a punishment and were 'helping' to take the awning down by batting the cables about and pouncing on anything else that moved, including Mr. N!

Well I told you I'd tell you all about everything that went on this weekend – now you probably wish I hadn't.. lol. Mum and Dad left after lunch, with Auntie Daph. I'm wondering what's going to happen tomorrow. Matron is bound to have told Ms. T that she saw M'selle dancing in the cabaret as Fifi, in exotic and extravagant dance mode with partner Fernando. No wonder she hasn't been at her best here during the day if she was dancing at night. Explains the feathers, too! Well, it's all going to be VERY interesting!!

Coo. This IS a long email. It's got paragraphs and everything!! Er.. are you still awake...? Hope all this rivettin' stuff hasn't bored you off to sleep! Love E.

Email : to l.purrsey@vsc.net **from** enid.p@setnet.com

Glad you got home safely. Still can't believe M'selle's been leading a double life. I'd love to have seen Polly Perkin's face when she recognised her at the club. It explains why M'selle hasn't been quite with it during the day, and it certainly explains all her solo rehearsals - and the feathers!! Glad you enjoyed the weekend - not quite what I anticipated .. lol. It'll be interesting to find out tomorrow what happens next. Loadsa love, E.

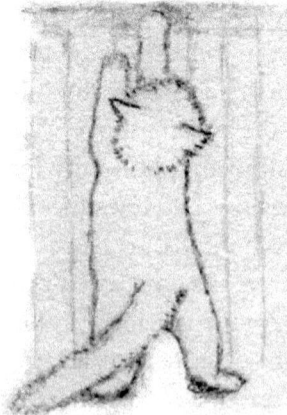

SIXTH FORM TEXTS :

Sam # Mamselle's gone AWOL.

Rosie # wot?

Immi # wot?

Yaz # wot?

Zo # wot?

Sam # That'll be because she's pregnant!

QUICK NOTE : TO ENID FROM TABITHA FELINE

ENID : URGENT. Would you type the attached and distribute it IMMEDI-ATELY to every member of staff BY HAND, interrupting classes where necessary. Thanks.

MEMO : TO ALL STAFF FROM TABITHA FELINE

IMPORTANT : PLEASE NOTE THAT THERE WILL BE A SHORT STAFF MEETING IN THE STAFF ROOM AT BREAK-TIME THIS MORNING. ALL STAFF ARE REQUIRED TO ATTEND. Classes can finish 10 minutes early.

Signed : Tabitha Feline

Email : to l.purrsey@vsc.net **and** moggym@topline.com **from** enid.p@ setnet.com

Dear Mum, Dad, Auntie Daph and Mogs. My phone's dead. Latest news. M'selle has left! Was last seen getting into a taxi with loads of luggage early on Sunday morning. The latest rumour is that she has run off with the dashing Fernando. Presumably after Matron and Auntie Daph saw her at the club. It's all happenin' here! Surely she must have known that someone would recognise her eventually. Lots of meetings and arrangements going on, and lots of gossip! But she's gone and that's that, and of course everything has to go on as normal. Loadsa love. E.

SIXTH FORM TEXTS :

Sam # Mamselle's run off to be a POLE DANCER called Fifi

Zo # wot?

Rosie # wot?

Yaz # wot?

Immi # wot?

NOTE TO ENID FROM TABITHA FELINE :

Enid : Would you type up the attached memo and distribute ASAP to ALL STAFF. Thanks.

MEMO : TO ALL STAFF FROM TABITHA FELINE

1. I shall speak briefly to the kittens at Assembly tomorrow morning simply to confirm that M'selle has left unexpectedly to pursue a career elsewhere, and that Form Tutors will hand out amended timetables shortly.
2. As mentioned at our meeting this morning, I should be glad to have your suggestions as to cover for M'selle's classes before I look for a temporary member of staff. Perhaps we could discuss the whole situation and any ideas you may have over sherry in my room, after dinner.

Tabitha Feline

SIXTH FORM TEXTS :

Rosie # we're on duty after dinner

Zo # why?

Yaz # Ms. T's doing sherry for the staff in her room

Immi # eeew!

Sam # aha but Catfood's made US cake. Yay!

MEMO : TO ALL STAFF FROM TABITHA FELINE

Thank you for your prompt response to my request for your suggestions in connection with cover for M'selle's classes. Although we will need to include some form of Performing Art, I agree that this is not a priority at present. I am particularly interested in Ms. Furlong's suggestion that we might consider navigation and orienteering skills. As both an indoor and outdoor activity, could this complement some of Ms. Kittsen's training sessions? Would you investigate this further and let me have specific details if you feel it is feasible. Thanks.

Tabitha Feline

SIXTH FORM TEXTS :

Immi # who do u think we'll have for dance now?

Zo # will we HAVE dance now?

Rosie # will we ever have dance again ha ha

Yaz # heard Ms. Mac say we might be havin public speaking instead

Sam # U mean public squeaking if its 1st yrs lol!

NOTE : TO TABITHA FROM PAWLENE MCFURLEY

I was very interested to read the Gazette's report of the Open Day, particularly their account of the Greek Dancing. Did you happen to hear the version M'selle gave to the Gazette reporter? It was difficult, of course, not to smile as the little ones counted their steps and swirls, trying to avoid each others' tails, but it was even more difficult not to smile at M'selle being dramatic and 'arty'! The kitlets when dancing are unfailingly sweet and endearing, of course, but expert they are not, which is part of their appeal as predictably, they got their veils tangled around their paws, their tails and each other. Matron and Ms. Mewsing's smooth expertise in swiftly extracting them, unravelling them, and setting them the right way up on their paws again, luckily avoided all the others being caught up in the melee. It's a good job the 5th Years are so adept at stepping over and round the kits - a skill which comes no doubt, from long practice and I was very impressed by their expertise. So I was really amused to hear M'selle's explanation of all this to the journalist. She moved immediately into her rather pretentious 'Arts and Art-speak' mode, vivaciously telling him that 'this Representational Art piece, entitled 'The Ties That Bind Us', depicts levels of aspiration and the struggle to rise to a higher plane despite the difficulties and setbacks of everyday existence', and so on. She very convincingly gave the impression that everything was all going exactly as she had originally envisaged - an imaginative and creative description which bore little resemblance to actual fact. I'm sure she believed every word of it at that moment - the absolute 'triumph of hope over experience'. The reporter, completely dazzled and obviously bowled over by M'selle's charm and bouffing and pouffing, was writing all this stuff down, thus he wasn't really watching the 1st Years being removed so they could be disentangled from their veils and each other, or the other little ones trying very hard not to fall over as they twirled about.

M'selle was very talented and had much to offer, but not all of it was practical or even remotely applicable to small and lively kits. Best to draw one of her veils over incidents like the Kitten Curtain!! See you at dinner. P.

Email : to l.purrsey@vsc.net **and** moggym@topline.com **from** enid.p@setnet.com

Dear Mum, Dad, Auntie Daph and Mogs. I'm putting a copy of the local paper, The Gazette, in the post. Open Day is front page news!! Loadsa love. E

PURRLEY AND DISTRICT GAZETTE

ST. CATTE'S ACADEMY LITERARY FESTIVAL AND OPEN DAY

Local dignitaries, members of the Town Council, well-known figures from the Academic world and many other visitors gathered at St. Catte's Academy for Kittens, to attend the Literary Festival and Open Day held each year at the Academy and in its gardens.

A display of Greek Dancing was given on the lawn by the 'Cattitudes'. The dancers moved down the paths to the centre lawn, where they performed a series of graceful, swirling, slow-moving sequences accentuated by their floating veils, and culminating in poses of statuesque stillness. At the same time, younger dancers moved among them, stepping and tumbling in a more spirited and fast-moving interpretation which involved weaving the veils around themselves and each other as they performed an abstract theme entitled 'The Ties that Bind Us'. M'selle Minou LaChatte who devised and choreographed the piece, explained that 'The duality of the dancing embodies the limitations we impose upon ourselves if we lack the confidence to take action and move forward. Performed simultaneously, the contrasting styles provide an apt comment on nature and modern life'. This was indeed, Representational Art at its most original.

The choir provided a soft and soulful background for the dancing, music which was melodious, moving and very atmospheric, and was composed by Ms. Mewsing, the choirmistress and conductor. The choir also gave a splendid performance later in the programme, singing a varied selection of pieces which ranged from traditional through classical to humorous, all of which was enjoyed immensely by the audience. The St. Catte's Chorus, the official title of the choir, recently performed in the 'Schools' Massed Choir Festival' at the Albert Hall.

In the newly-built outdoor training facility in the Academy grounds, the Aerial Athletic and Extended Leap team demonstrated their extraordinary talents and fitness as with superb skill and dexterity, they achieved amazing feats of strength and balance. They are trained by Catlin Kittsen, Bronze Medallist in the recent Olympuss Games. It is not difficult to see why this team, formed comparatively recently, qualified for the Area Aerial Athletics and Extended Leap Finals, in which they will compete next month.

The Academy's Literary Festival performances of 'King Ear' by the Third and Fourth Year pupils, and 'A Tail of Two Kitties' by the First and Second Years, were presented in the open air theatre erected for the occasion in order to take advantage of the excellent weather. The Sixth Form had devised and written their own play, 'A Midsummer Fright's Scream', which was ingenious, well acted and very funny.

There were the usual classroom displays of work accomplished during the term, and the gardens were at their seasonal best. 'We had just as much rain as we needed,' said Mr. N. Nepeta, in whose hands the gardens and grounds flourish, 'and not enough to ruin the floral displays.'

Dr. Tabitha Feline CBE, Principal, said ' Our Literary Festival and Open Day has been very successful, and the St. Catte's pupils and staff have every reason to be proud of their achievements'.

Refreshments were provided by Mrs. D. Catford and her staff, to the usual high standards, and were appreciated by all who attended, including Sir Mortimer Morris, M.P., the Mayor, His Worship Roy Bethes, representatives from the Town Council, the Academy Governors and well-known figures from the Academic world.

See Page 4 for photographs, further details and a full list of attendees.

QUICK NOTE TO PAWLENE McFURLEY AND POLLY PURRKINS FROM TABITHA FELINE : URGENT. Minim Mewsing has been to see me. Could you pop in ASAP T.

SIXTH FORM TEXTS :

Yaz # Mamselle Fifi is apache dancing in a club in Paris with partner Fernando

Immi # OMG

Sam # probably not pregnant then

Rosie # It's Ms. Mewsing who's pregnant, heard her tell Matron

Zo # wot?

Sam # wot?

Immi # wot?

Yaz # wot?

MEMO : TO MS. TABITHA FELINE FROM CATLIN KITTSEN AND PHOEBE FURLONG

As requested, we have explored the feasibility of adding Navigation and Orienteering Skills to the curriculum and feel that this could be too specific. Possibly giving the kittens a broader experience - to include aspects of survival, woodcraft and tracking skills might be more suitable? Could we arrange a meeting to give you the details? P. Furlong and C. Kittsen

MEMO : TO MS. P. FURLONG AND MS. C. KITTSEN FROM TABITHA FELINE

Thank you for your speedy response in connection with new classes. I shall be interested to hear your ideas, and Enid will arrange a meeting for when you have free time today.

Tabitha Feline

NOTE TO PAWLENE AND POLLY FROM TABITHA FELINE : Phoebe Furlong and Catlin have come up with some interesting ideas. Instead of 'Navigation and Orienteering', they sre suggesting a modified version which they have called 'Orientation and Survival skills'. Also, Minim Mewsing says she has a friend who could replace her while she is on Caternity Leave. Could we discuss later. Sherry? T.

SIXTH FORM TEXTS :

Rosie # OMG we've got to do survival skills

Immi # wot? Instead of dance ?

Zo # sleepin in plastic bags?

Sam # without food?

Zo # we'd have to catch our own

Immi # wot? outside?

Yaz # we'd get wet

Sam # I'd rather do Mamselle's frouffy dancin'

MEMO : TO MS. TABITHA FELINE FROM MS. CATLIN KITTSEN AND MS. PHOEBE FURLONG

ORIENTATION AND SURVIVAL SKILLS : Further to our meeting yesterday, we have produced an outline of the course which if you approve, could be distributed with the Agenda for discussion at the Staff Meeting. We have given a brief description of the proposed activities and an outline for timetabling - possibly an introductory week of tuition then trial outdoor sessions to take advantage of the present fine weather. This would be followed by an afternoon of practical activity, on the lines of the recent fun-run but requiring path-finding and sign-recognition, therefore utilising the skills learned in the earlier sessions. On-going classes would be integrated into the normal timetable.

Phoebe Furlong

Catlin Kittsen

Email : to l.purrsey@vsc.net **and** moggym@topline.com **from** enid.p@setnet.com

Hi Mum, Dad, Auntie Daph and Mogs. Well, I thought once Open Day was over, it would be quiet and we'd be back to normal, but there's all sorts of things going on. M'selle's mysterious and abrupt departure obviously meant we were short staffed, so all sorts of hasty arrangements had to be made to cover her classes. Dance is definitely not on the agenda at the moment until we have someone to teach it, so it looks as if Catlin Kittsen and Phoebe Furlong will be introducing survival and orienteering sessions. I'm not absolutely sure of the details yet, but not even the biggest optimist is likely to turn the kits loose in the countryside with just a map, and a plastic bag to sleep in. All will be made clear after the Staff Meeting, no doubt. The 6th Form's latest gossip about M'selle is that she and the dashing Fernando are apache dancers in Paris! Apparently, apache dancing is a vigorous and slightly violent form of dance in pairs and typically French, so the 6th Form tell me, and they know all about it because they looked it up! And their other BIG piece of news is that it's Ms. Mewsing who's pregnant, not M'selle! Now THAT was a surprise. They knew all about it well before it was announced - they're like the eyes and ears of the world!! Anyway, there it is! Ms. Mewsing will be going on Caternity Leave quite soon. Nobody knew anything about it, and she was doing all sorts of extra work taking dance rehearsals as well as the choir and loads of extra stuff for Open Day! She was quite concerned to be adding to the staff chaos M'selle left behind. I'm arranging interviews for Ms. Mewsing's Caternity Leave cover, and of course, we'll be having a new member of staff to replace M'selle, so at the moment, there's loads to do. Mogs – glad to hear you're feeling better, and hope to see you this weekend. Love to all. E.

SIXTH FORM TEXTS :

Yaz # Catlin's asked if we will take the little ones map-reading

Sam # wot, outside? It's raining

Rosie # indoors, I've got the maps

Immi # bit like a treasure hunt then

Zo # with no treasure lol

MEMO : TO MRS. DORA CATFORD FROM TABITHA FELINE

Thanks for agreeing to provide coffee and cake for Friday's meeting at 10 a.m. in the Staff Room, when I shall be introducing our new members of staff, Ms. Kitty Tailor and Ms. Chloe Pawson. **Tabitha**

MEMO : TO FORM TUTORS AND ALL STAFF FROM TABITHA FELINE

I shall be formally introducing our two new members of staff, Ms. Kitty Tailor and Ms. Chloe Pawson, at Assembly on Friday morning. Afterwards, at 10 a.m. Mrs. Catford will provide her excellent coffee and cake in the Staff Room. I feel a brief, informal get-together is appropriate, so they can meet us all. I know you will give them a warm welcome and will provide all the assistance they may need.

Tabitha Feline

SIXTH FORM TEXTS :

Sam # to Rosie #, Zo #, Immi #, Yaz # I've volunteered us to serve the coffee in the Staff Room on Friday after Assembly. Yay....cake !

Email : to l.purrsey@vsc.net **and** moggym@topline.com **from** enid.p@setnet.com

Hello, everybody. How's things. All's well here. Two new members of staff have started so I'm not the new one any more. It's funny, I feel as if I've been here forever. It's great to be showing THEM the ropes. They both seem very nice. Things were quiet until the 1st Yrs were doing their first map-reading exercise. Indoors because it was raining. The route around the school was marked out and they had maps, and had to check in with the 6th Form at certain points so they didn't wander off. It all went amazingly well until the final head-count at the end, when they discovered that Sofronia and Sapphira were missing. The others went in for tea while we looked for them. Mr. Nepeta eventually found them in the boiler room, climbing all over the pipes chasing spiders and then they mewed and moaned and complained because they'd got all cobwebby! They'd apparently had their map upside down! Instead of going up the stairs, they'd gone down. Catlin made us laugh as she wrote a large note to herself 'Remember to mark TOP: THIS WAY UP on each map' for when they do their first real map reading/orientation session in the grounds next week. Love, E.

QUICK NOTE : TO PAWLENE FROM TABITHA : There appears to be quite an interest in the orienteering/map-reading event tomorrow. Have had a quick word with Catlin and Phoebe and they seem to have everything in hand. T.

NOTE : TO TABITHA FROM PAWLENE : It all seems to be well organised: enough staff at designated checkpoints, different routes clearly marked for different ability groups, as much independent work as possible for each group, supervision appears adequate, Sixth Form on 'roving scout' duty to move around and keep an eye on things. Er - what could possibly go wrong??? **P.**

Email : to l.purrsey@vsc.net **and** moggym@topline.com **from** enid.p@
setnet.com

HI Mum, Dad, Auntie Daph and Mogs. How's things? Hope you're all ok and sorry I missed your call last night, Mum, I was late getting home. We had the first map-reading orientation event today and you wouldn't believe how much organisation had been put in to make sure it went smoothly, as all the kittens were involved although they followed different routes depending on which year they were in. It started off really well. The little ones, clutching their maps, went off on their route supervised by Phoebe Furlong, and then the other groups got their maps and they set off at intervals. Even Pawlene McFurley said how well the organisation was working, and she's not easily impressed. The 1st Yrs. got back first as they had the shortest, easiest route, and the other groups arrived when they'd completed their course. Then Ms. T came down and said that from her office window she could see what appeared to be a surfeit of kittens on the lawn, with still more streaming in through the gates. There were kittens everywhere. Unbelievable numbers of them - reading maps, queueing up for Mrs. Catford's refreshments, chasing around, pouncing on each other and generally milling about and causing confusion and chaos. More kittens in one place than anyone would have thought possible and still more coming in and they definitely weren't ours! Nobody had any idea where they were all coming from! Then the 6th Form appeared in the background, very ruffled and breathless, directing yet more kittens in, and they then formed a barrier across the gate so no-one could get out. All was tumult for a bit, but it turned out that the kittens from St. Thomas School were doing a hearty cross-country run and our 6th Form, seeing kittens OUTSIDE the gates when all our kittens should be INSIDE the gates, went out and herded every kitten they could see back inside before they got lost, just to be on the safe side, so the rest of the St. Thomas' runners followed them in and we ended up with all of them - far too many kittens for comfort. Absolutely hordes of kittens, swarming everywhere. Order was eventually restored when the St. Thomas' staff puffed in, some-what bemused as to why their kittens had ended up here. They rounded their lot up, sorted them out, marshalled them into groups and despatched them back on their cross-country way, and everyone relaxed and heaved a sigh of relief. Then we discovered that we'd lost the 1st Years! Nightmare! So a search party had to go off and hurtle after the St. Thomas's lot just in case they'd got mixed up with them. They hadn't. We knew they had originally been counted in back here, so we had yet more search parties everywhere, frantically looking into every nook and cranny. In the end, they were found fast asleep in a heap in their cuddle basket. They'd got so tired they'd put themselves to bed, half of them still muddy and clutching their maps. And guess who was in there with them? Young Bill! Who used to be Belle!!! Ms. T 'phoned Dr. Felix, of course, and they decided that extracting a sleepy kit would mean that the whole basketful would have been awake and fractious, so he was returned to St. Thomas's next morning. Talk about never a dull moment! Everyone's exhausted! Speak to you soon. Loadsa love, E.

SIXTH FORM TEXTS :

Yaz # OMG did you ever see so many kittens

Immi # nightmare numbers

Sam # never want to see another kitten ever again

Zo # one cat per home is quite enough

Rosie # hope Ms. Mewsing doesn't feel that way , given present circumstances lol

INVITATION :

TO ALL MEMBERS OF THE SIXTH FORM I should be very pleased if THE ST. CATTE'S SIXTH FORM STUDENTS would join me for tea in my room at 3 p.m. tomorrow afternoon. I look forward to seeing you.

Tabitha Feline

QUICK NOTE TO PAWLENE AND POLLY FROM TABITHA: Just to let you know that I have invited the Sixth Form for tea tomorrow afternoon in order to thank them for their sterling work yesterday, and of course, I hope you will join us. T.

ACCEPTANCE :

TO DR. TABITHA FELINE

THE MEMBERS OF ST. CATTE'S SIXTH FORM

HAVE PLEASURE IN ACCEPTING DR. TABITHA FELINE'S

KIND INVITATION TO TEA

IN HER ROOM AT 3 p.m. THIS AFTERNOON

SIXTH FORM TEXTS :

Sam # coo, tea with Ms. T

Rosie # do u think it's about dance?

Immi # wot dance

Zo # OMG nooooooooooooo

Yaz # we're doing dance again ?

Sam # I'M NOT

Rosie # notice in the main hall

Zo # c u there in a mo.

NOTICE
PROGRESSIVE MOVEMENT
CLASSES WILL BE HELD IN THE GYMNASIUM.
WOULD ANY KITTEN INTERESTED
PLEASE SEE MS. TAILOR

QUICK NOTE TO PAWLENE FROM TABITHA FELINE : The kits are doing a lot of hopping and skipping about suddenly. I assume this is in response to Ms. Tailor's Progressive Movement classes. Now that we have all more or less recovered from the influx of extra kittens and Mr. Nepeta has almost restored the lawn and flower beds, can I take it that these classes will be held indoors at the moment? T.

NOTE : TO TABITHA FELINE FROM P. McFURLEY, DEPUTY HEAD.

Ms. Tailor's Progressive Movement classes have proved very popular with the 3rd and 4th Year kittens. She is keen to give the sessions more structure, and suggests that Morris Dancing would be suitable. I notice that progress along the corridors is certainly brisker than of late. Discuss over dinner? **P.**

SIXTH FORM TEXTS :

Sam # IT'S MORRIS DANCING!

Rosie # Are they MAD

Zo # wot, you mean bells and everything?

Yaz # kitlets with bells nooooooooooo

Immi # Ms. T didn't mention morris dancing during tea

Rosie # OMG we need to see Catlin

Email : to l.purrsey@vsc.net **and** moggym@topline.com **from** enid.p@setnet.com

Hiya. How's everyone? Glad you're feeling o.k. now, Mogs. When are you coming down? I'm hoping to be home this weekend so we can start organising something. Everything seems to be going remarkably smoothly here. No news really, which is a relief! The new staff are settling in, and Ms. Tailor has very daringly started dance up again. Progressive Movement, but actually it's Morris dancing! The Cattitudes are still languidly drooping and oozing about, without veils but with all the tossings of the head and bouffing and frouffings of the tail a la M'selle, and they are resolutely refusing to stoop to Ms. Tailor's Morris dancing ideas. The 3rd and 4th Years have taken to it in a big way. Ms. T. okayed me ordering the bells and ribbons and now the kits are tinkling and twinkling all over the place. The 1st Yrs joined in of course but they spend their time chasing about patting the bells, trying to chew the ribbons, pouncing on each other and generally looking cute. Ms. Tailor doesn't seem to mind. The 3rd and 4th Yrs absolutely adore her and gaggles of them trail about after her. The stairs and corridors don't get as clogged up as they did, although with the Cattitudes still draping themselves all over the place and the Morris Mews (as they insist upon calling themselves), jogging and bobbing along at a much faster pace than the Cattitudes, there are pile-ups at times but no real problems. Of course the Cattitudes as they pose and drift, do not take kindly to getting swept along on a surge of jolly Morris movements, so there is the odd stand-off, but nothing serious. Did I say I'll be taking time off as soon as this term finishes, so will be home for a week soon? Loadsa love, E

Enid : The end of term looms and I need to finish preparation for my final Assembly Address to the kittens on the last morning. Would you open a file for my ideas and rough notes. They are rather random at the moment, so if you would just type them up as they are, I can make use of them, as, when and if, I need them, and put them into some sort of order later. Thanks. TF.

DR. TABITHA FELINE : NOTES : END OF YEAR ASSEMBLY

INTRODUCTION

THANKS TO :

Sixth Form: for vigilance and sterling work in supervision duties; responsible, reliable etc. etc

All staff : for taking on extra work and responsibilities during the year, clubs, competitions etc.

M'selle : Although no longer with us, I should like to thank her for all her work, particularly for all her preparation for the memorable Open Day dance display.

Ms. Mewsing: for Choir, Festival, taking dance and drama rehearsals etc. Hopefully by then we will have had news of birth and number in litter.

ALL HOLIDAY TASKS must be completed. In particular YOU MUST PRACTICE :

The Silent Miaow - one of the most powerful weapons we have, communicating as it does utter helplessness, deep unhappiness, and a need so profound that we are unable even able to express ourselves vocally. It is a non-cry - of longing and desperation that affects even the hardest Human heart and instantly evokes feelings of pity and protectiveness. Effective for persuasion, particularly in overcoming any resistance should you decide to take up residence with a Human who appears to show reluctance. Can be used judiciously if you are put outside at night or indeed, at any other time, or if you wish to have a door opened when your Human is otherwise occupied or sitting down comfortably, or when you wish to be fed food from someone's plate or the dinner table. Practice this, perfect it, AND NEVER EVER OVER-USE IT, or it will lose its effectiveness.

Good manners - require us sometimes to compromise on something which we know is ours by right, and even allow us to accede gracefully to a specific request from our Human, without us losing face or our authority. Trained properly by you, your Human will understand that **UNLESS YOU CHOOSE TO,** you do not come when called, or allow yourself to be picked up or cuddled, or sit on a lap unless you wish to. However, if your Human is sad, lonely or needy in some other way, it is only good manners to acknowledge this and help by instigating close contact, purring and relaxing on the lap as for as long as you think it is required, accepting the intimacy and caresses, and possibly giving the hand or face a lick if you feel it is necessary, to show that you empathise.

Never, ever let your Humans down in front of visitors - do what is requested of you, come when called, be utterly charming and entertaining. When the guests leave, then you can assert yourself firmly. Remember kittens, you have dignity - stand upon it!

Gifts – a caring gesture and much appreciated. Your Human will react very noisily and will rush around spectacularly in gratitude, particularly if you choose a rat. Voles, shrews and mice are received more quietly. A live gift causes great excitement, but bringing one in will probably result in you being put out. Why is a mystery. Don't kill birds, the indoor versions or the outdoor ones, or if you do, don't bring them home

Oh, and never leave a Gift on your Human's bed. For some reason, they don't like it. If you do decide to show your affection in this way, expect very noisy displays of excitement and gratitude. Good when you want attention, but not conducive to the rest and recuperation required after a concentrated hunting session.

Attitudes - I cannot emphasise enough the importance of friendly bearing, pretty poses, being mysterious, being captivating etc. etc. As an example: raise your tail when greeting your Human like a little flagpole of affection, or regard, or goodwill, and you will raise your Human's spirits. The reason for this is another mystery and has no explanation, but it is fact. ? Give more examples?

Affection - St. Catte's kittens have no difficulty in showing and receiving affection, as training your Human is only accomplished with love, dedication and care. ...etc. Remember – a Happy Human is a Trained Human, trained by you to provide a well organised and comfortable home – for you, and which is run to YOUR catisfaction.

Discipline - Using 'The Stare' as a reprimand. N.B. NEVER forget the power of 'The Stare'. Inducing guilt. Using the ignoring technique Refusing inferior food. Drying yourself on the bed if you've been left out in the rain ...etc. etc

Motherhood - A wonderful thing. I had my kittens, wouldn't have missed it: fun, wonder, deeply satisfying - but someone else can have the next lot. ? (needs rephrasing?) There have to be kittens or there would be no cats. Someone has to have the kittens. It does not have to be you. Not if you want to run your own home and bring up a Human family, training them the way they should be trained to provide a best possible environment for you, which will of course, benefit them as well. We are Queen Cats, females able to breed. The word comes from the Ancient English word 'quean', the meaning of which refers to the enthusiasm with which some queens approached the whole process of mating. This does not have to be you. As Domestic Goddess Supreme, which we were in ancient Egypt, you will be in sole charge of your establishment: The Perfect House Cat, with everything running to your satisfaction. Just imagine the huge upset of introducing a litter of helpless mewling little creatures, requiring feeding, training and a lot of care and attention 24/7 for many weeks. You will be completely occupied with all this on your own, as well as with the constant vigilance of keeping your clutch of kittens from under the feet of your Humans, and hauling them off chairs before your Humans sit down and squash them. Humans are creatures of habit and do not really like their routines changed – they get fractious and lax and will forget your household rules. And kittens need homes, so you will always wonder where they are and if your training successfully equipped them to become The Domestic Cat Supreme.

Or - and this has to be considered and taken into account - your Humans may react to your pregnancy with enthusiasm, cater for your every whim, adore the appealing sight of you with your little ones, and decide to keep all of them. In which case YOU will now be living in a home with FOUR, FIVE OR SIX cats, where previously there was just one - you! IS THIS WHAT YOU WANT?

So remember - canoodling leads to kittens, kittens can happen to anyone, AND THEY FREQUENTLY DO. Dalliance is diverting but invariably ends in disaster - and kittens. Motherhood is normal and natural, but not necessarily a good idea. SO - GET SPAYED BEFORE YOU GET LAID. However, resourceful though we are, spaying is not always possible as the decision to arrange this is not in your paws. SO - resist his blandishments, no matter how devastatingly attractive he is, no matter how handsome his whiskers. Resist nature's call. JUST SAY NO.

CONCLUSION : We have behind us a very successful year. You, as St. Catte's kittens, can be proud of our Aerial Athletics and Extended Leap team, thanks to Ms. Kittsen; proud of our choir, thanks to Ms. Mewsing and at present Ms. Pawson; and proud of yourselves and your collective efforts in presenting our Literary Festival and Open Day, when the standard you achieved was extremely high. St. Cattes's is proud of YOU. Enjoy your vacation and return refreshed and invigorated, ready for the new term.

N.B. Mention all staff by name.

My thanks to you all, etc.

SIXTH FORM TEXTS :

Sam # Quick. Back windows. Mrs. Catford's putting suitcases into Mr. Nepeta's car. THEY'RE ELOPING!!!

Rosie # wot?

Zo # wot?

Yaz # wot?

Immi # wot?

Email : to l.purrsey@vsc.net **and** moggym@topline.com **from** enid.p@ setnet.com

OMG. Latest 6th Form rumour. Mrs. Catford and Mr. Nepeta have run away together. Eloped! THE SIXTH FORM ARE SUCH LITTLE GOSSIPS!!!! See you at the weekend. Loadsa love, E.

P.S. Oooooooooo! Can't help wondering if they MIGHT BE RIGHT, lol !!!!

* 9 7 8 1 9 1 0 7 5 7 7 6 5 *